Grammar Plus

【Second Edition】

大学英語『グラマー・プラス』

【改訂新版】

Andrew E. Bennett

Toru Komiya

NAN'UN-DO

このテキストの音声を無料で視聴（ストリーミング）・ダウンロードできます。自習用音声としてご活用ください。
以下のサイトにアクセスしてテキスト番号で検索してください。

https://nanun-do.com　テキスト番号 [**512152**]

※ 無線 LAN（WiFi）に接続してのご利用を推奨いたします。

※ 音声ダウンロードは Zip ファイルでの提供になります。
　お使いの機器によっては別途ソフトウェア（アプリケーション）の導入が必要となります。

音声ファイル
無料 DL
のご案内

Grammar Plus【Second Edition】音声ダウンロードページは
左記の QR コードからもご利用になれます。

Read by
Anya Floris
Chris Koprowski

本書の目的と構成

英語学習者にとって、文法は強力なツールとなります。時制やさまざまな品詞、そのほかの文法項目を学習することで、他者の考えを理解しながら、自分の言いたいことを口に出したり書いたりすることができるようになります。その一方で、文法は、単に決まりごとや規則を集めたものではありません。それは言語空間をすみずみまで満たし、私たちが読み、書き、聞き、話すことすべての中に存在します。言うなれば、文法こそ言語の血液なのです。

そこで登場するのが本書『Grammar Plus』です。本書は、英語の主要な文法項目を漏れなく扱う30のユニットで構成されています。それぞれの文法項目を説明するために実用的な例文が写真やイラストとともに掲載されているので、それが長く記憶にとどまります。さらに、文法を、読む、書く、聞く、話す、という4技能を通して身につけます。この総合的なアプローチによって、英語の基本的な運用能力を強化しながら、日常生活で文法がどのように使われるのか学びます。本書は、文法の学習が楽しく、実用的で、達成感を感じられるものになることを意図して作られています。

以下は、Grammar Plusのそれぞれのユニットを構成する要素の説明です。

文法項目を学ぶときは、最初に基本的な文の構造に注目することが大切です。そのため、『Grammar Plus』では、各ユニットの最初の2ページに基本的な知識を掲載しています。

ほとんどのユニットでは、学習する文法項目は3つのカテゴリに分けられています。たとえば、右に示したユニット(Unit 6：進行形)では、カテゴリは「現在進行形」「過去進行形」「進行形の疑問文」となっています。

まず、それぞれのカテゴリには3つの例文があり、文法項目が実際に使われる場面に対応した写真が添えられています。その下には、さらに3〜4つの 例文とその日本語訳が示されています。最後に、文法項目の働きと用法の説明があります。

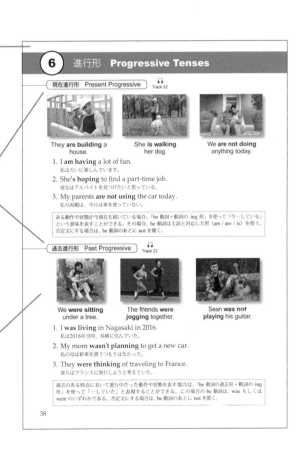

例文を読み上げている音声は、データをダウンロードして聞くことができます。そのトラック番号は、ヘッドフォンのアイコンの下に示されています。

進行形の疑問文　Asking Questions Track 24

Are you **leaving**? What are you **cooking**? Were they **using** the boat?

1. **Are** you still **taking** photography classes?
   あなたは今も写真教室に参加しているのですか。
2. **Were** you **working** in the garden all morning?
   あなたは午前中ずっと庭仕事をしていたのですか。
3. **Was** Carl **trying** to contact me yesterday?
   カールは昨日、私に連絡を取ろうとしていたのですか。

現在形でも過去形でも、進行形の疑問文を作る場合は「be 動詞＋主語＋動詞」の語順となる。また、What や Where などの疑問詞で始まる疑問文は、さらにその疑問詞を文頭に置く。

Grammar Exercises

Ⓐ　（　　）内の指示に従って、次の文を書き換えなさい。

[例] I was resting.（現在進行形に）→ <u>I am resting.</u>

1. They cleaned their rooms.（過去進行形に）
   _____

2. We are watching TV.（否定文に）
   _____

3. Where do you live now?（現在進行形に）
   _____

4. He studies psychology.（現在進行形に）
   _____

5. We are trying our best.（過去進行形に）
   _____

39

Grammar Exercisesのセクションには、3種類の演習問題が掲載されています。ここでは、多肢選択問題、動詞の活用問題、誤り訂正問題、文の書き換え問題など、さまざまな種類の問題が用意されています。いずれの問題も、各ユニットの文法項目についての知識を確認し、その知識を使うことの自信を深め、論理的・客観的な思考力を養うことを目的としています。

Ⓑ　（　　）内に示された動詞と時制を使って、進行形の文を作りなさい。

[例] We _____ _____.（study・現在）→ We <u>are</u> <u>studying</u>.

1. She _____ _____.（sleep・現在）

2. All of my friends _____ _____.（dance・過去）

3. Bob and Kate _____ _____ _____.（play・過去＋否定）

4. One of us _____ _____.（go・現在）

5. What _____ you _____?（do・過去）

Ⓒ　次の会話文の空欄に適当な語を入れなさい。

1. A: Hi, Rudolfo. Where (　　　) you (　　　)?
   B: Hey, Emily. I'm going to the supermarket.

2. A: Are you still helping Aaron?
   B: Yes, I (　　　) (　　　) him study for the test.

3. A: Kim looked sick yesterday morning. Was she feeling all right?
   B: No, she (　　　) (　　　) (　　　) well. She went to the clinic in the afternoon.

Skill Building

Ⓐ Listening　3つの文(A, B, C)を聞き、それぞれの内容と一致しているイラストの下にその記号を書きなさい。 Track 25

1. _____   2. _____   3. _____

40

リスニングの課題では。学習者は一連のイラストを見ながら、いくつかの文を読み上げている音声を聞きます。録音されているそれぞれの文の冒頭には、「A」「B」「C」などの文字が付けられています。それぞれのイラストの下には数字が書かれています。学習者は、イラストを正しく説明する文の文字を書き留めます。（文を読み上げる音声データはダウンロード可能）

B Speaking　次の会話文を読み、以下のリストから適切な単語を選んで空欄を埋めなさい。

| are | is | am | were | was |

Mitsuko:　Sorry I couldn't see you yesterday. I was in Sapporo all day.

Hiro:　That's all right. What ₁(　　　) you doing there?

Mitsuko:　I ₂(　　　) visiting my uncle in the hospital.

Hiro:　I'm sorry to hear that. Is it serious?

Mitsuko:　No, he just had a skiing accident. He ₃(　　　) getting better now. Also, my mother and sister ₄(　　　) taking turns making his meals. They visit him every day.

Hiro:　That's so nice of them! Actually, I ₅(　　　) hoping to visit Sapporo soon. Maybe we can go together.

質問の答えとして最も適切なものを選びなさい。

1. (　) Who went skiing in Sapporo?
　　A: Hiro　　　　　　　　　　B: Mitsuko
　　C: Hiro's sister　　　　　　D: Mitsuko's uncle

2. (　) What does Hiro suggest doing?
　　A: Going skiing with some friends
　　B: Traveling to Sapporo with Mitsuko
　　C: Visiting a classmate in the hospital
　　D: Making a meal for a relative

C Writing　(　　) 内の単語を並べ替え、正しい文を作りなさい。

1. She (home / driving / is / now).

　　_____

2. The model (wearing / not / jewelry / was).

　　_____

3. Are (for / joining / they / dinner / us)?

　　_____

41

その次はスピーキングの課題です。ここには2人の人物による会話文があり、その中に5つの空欄が設けられています。学習者は、与えられているリストの中から、最適と思われる単語や語句を、それぞれの空欄に記入します(リスト中の単語や語句は1回しか使えないことに注意)。この課題では、各ユニットの文法項目が普段の自然な会話の中でどのように使われるのかを確認します。

この演習問題は、学習者がどれだけダイアログを理解できたのか確認します。学習者はそれぞれの質問に最適な答えを選びます。

最後は作文の練習です。あるユニットでは、文と文の結合や文の書き換えなどの練習問題が、また別のユニットでは、並べ替え問題が用意されています。いくつかの問題では、文の一部の単語がヒントとして与えられています。

このセクションでの目標は、学習者に各ユニットで学ぶ文法項目を使った興味深い文章(物語や記事)を楽しんで読んでもらうことです。それぞれの文章には文法問題が組み込まれています。問題の形式は、多肢選択問題、動詞の活用問題、並び替え問題などです。文章の下には語注があり、読解に役立つほか、追加情報も掲載しています。

文章の後には正誤問題があり、学習者の理解度を確認します。

— **Grammar Through Reading** —

A Reading Passage　[　]内の動詞を進行形に変えて、それぞれの空欄に入れなさい。

In many countries, people love Japanese comics, cartoons, and toys. Pop culture items are sold at stores and online. ₁Thanks to pop culture, many Japanese terms (　　　　) (　　　　) [enter] the English language. ₂People (　　　　) (　　　　) [use] words like "manga" and "anime" in daily life. In fact, for more than half a century, many of the world's most famous cartoons and characters have come from Japan.

Some overseas fans watch anime in Japanese. The shows often have English subtitles on the bottom. Other people prefer listening to English versions of the shows. For manga, most fans read English translations. A few prefer the original versions. It's a fun way to learn Japanese. ₃One thing is certain: Japanese pop culture (　　　　) (　　　　) [become] very popular!

NOTES　comic「漫画本」 cartoon「アニメ」 pop culture「大衆文化」 item「商品」
term「ことば」 daily「毎日の」 show「番組」 subtitle「字幕」 translation「翻訳」
certain「明らかな」

B Comprehension　それぞれの文の内容が正しければ T(true) を、誤りであれば F(false) を○で囲みなさい。

1. The article does not mention buying items from friends.　　T　F

2. The word "anime" is used outside of Japan.　　T　F

3. Manga is always read in Japanese.　　T　F

42

和訳問題では、学習者は文章の中にある3つの文を日本語に訳します。訳す文には下線が引かれ、冒頭に番号が付いています。

なお、各ユニットの最後には、Reference Material（参考資料）として、そのユニットで学習する文法項目に関連する追加情報が表やリスト、追加の説明、例文などの形で掲載されており、学習者はさらに理解を深めることができます。

C Translation 前ページの英文の中で、下線が引かれている文を日本語に訳しなさい。

1. _____

2. _____

3. _____

Reference Material

動詞の -ing 形の作り方　Chart of Progressive Form Spelling Rules

動詞の種類	規則	例	
一般的な動詞	-ing を付ける	lift attend	lifting attending
語尾が発音しない e で終わる動詞	e を除いて -ing を付ける	make drive	making driving
語尾が ie で終わる動詞	ie を除いて -ying を付ける	tie lie	tying lying
語尾が「子音＋強調される母音＋子音」で終わる動詞	最後の1文字を追加してから -ing を付ける	run submit	running submitting
語尾が「子音＋強調されない母音＋子音」で終わる動詞	-ing を付ける	visit limit	visiting limiting
語尾が w, x, y で終わる動詞	-ing を付ける	fix try	fixing trying

1. My son **is attending** a small kindergarten.
2. For the group lunch, **are** you **making** an appetizer or a dessert?
3. Let's try to be quiet. Dad **is lying down** in his bedroom.
4. **Are** you **planning** to buy a new washing machine?
5. The store **is limiting** purchases to one per person.
6. Sorry, I didn't hear you. I **was sawing up** some firewood.

第2版での変更点

『Grammar Plus第2版』には、旧版からの改良点がいくつかあります。新たなユニットが6つ追加され、全30ユニット構成となりました。これらのユニットの追加により、カバーする重要な文法項目の範囲が広がり、本書はより総合的な文法学習教材となりました。元からあるユニットはすべて改訂し、内容、量ともに拡張されました。

第2版では、各ユニットは 6 ページになりました。学習する文法項目のすべてに、写真付きの例文を3つずつ用意しています（初版では写真が3枚だったのが 6〜9枚に増加）。また、追加の例文には新たにその日本語訳が追加され、学習者のための便宜を図っています。

ほかにもさまざまな変更が、本書全体を通して行われています。スピーキングの演習には、理解度の確認問題が追加されています。リーディング課題の文章には、学習者の興味を引くような画像が追加されました。また、各ユニットの参考資料は巻末から、ユニットの最後のページに移動し、これを機に多くのユニットで情報が更新されています。

同時に改訂された教師用マニュアルには、本書の演習問題の解答と録音されている英文が掲載されています。関連データを収めたCDや追加の音声データなどの教師用資料も南雲堂から入手できます。

改訂新版の刊行に際し、小宮徹氏、マイケル・クリチェリー氏、加藤敦氏、および南雲堂編集チームの皆様の多大なご助力に感謝いたします。質・量ともこれだけ充実した文法書を制作できたのも、関係者全員の情熱、努力、専門知識の賜です。

『Grammar Plus』をご利用の先生方へ:

本書をお選びいただき、誠にありがとうございます。先生方の授業の成功をお祈りするとともに、本書によって英語学習がさらに楽しく効果のあるものとなることを願っております。

本書で学習する学生の皆さんへ:

常に ベストを尽くしましょう。文法を学ぶ目的は、他者の考えを理解し自分が伝えたいことを表現するのに役立つ道具を手に入れるためであることを忘れないでください。皆さんは未来の世界のリーダーです。皆さんが自分の意見を自由に英語で発信できるようになることを期待しています。

楽しい英語学習を!

アンドルー E.ベネット

CONTENTS

様子や状態を表す（be ＋ (副詞＋) 形容詞）　Describing Appearances and States

 Track 2

She **is** surprised.

He **is** happy.

The road **is** closed.

1. I **am** tired. 私は疲れました。

2. He **is not** hungry. 彼は空腹ではない。

3. **Are** they ready yet? もう準備はできましたか。

4. Mr. Nelson **is** very smart. ネルソンさんはとても賢い。

be 動詞の現在形には am、are、is があり、主語が I のときは am を、you と they そして名詞の複数には are を、he、she、it そして単数の名詞には is を使う。否定文は be 動詞のあとに not を置いて作り、疑問文は主語と be 動詞の順番を逆にして作る。「主語 ＋ be 動詞 ＋ (副詞＋) 形容詞」という文では、その主語となっている人や物の様子や状態を表すことができる。

事実を述べる（be ＋名詞 (句)　Giving Information

 Track 3

They **are** good friends.

It **is** an elephant.

They **aren't** doctors.

1. We **are** brothers. 僕たちは兄弟です。

2. It **is not** my jacket. それは私のジャケットではありません。

3. **Are** you a nurse? あなたは看護士ですか。

4. **It's** a long movie. それは長編映画です。

「主語 ＋ be 動詞 ＋ 名詞 (句)」という文では、「主語 ＝ 述語」つまり「… (主語) は… (名詞) である」という情報を伝えることができる。

時間や場所などを示す（be ＋前置詞句／副詞） Indicating Locations, Times, etc.

The ducks **are** in the pond.

The clock **is** on the wall.

The wedding **is** today.

1.	The party **is** on Friday.	そのパーティーは金曜日にあります。
2.	Larry **isn't** from Canada.	ラリーはカナダ出身ではありません。
3.	**Is** the sugar in the box?	砂糖はその箱の中にありますか。
4.	Our big test **is** tomorrow.	大事なテストが明日あります。

be 動詞のあとに、日時や場所を表す語句を続けると、あることが起こる時間や、何かが存在する場所などを言い表すことができる。その語句には「前置詞＋名詞」または副詞が使われる。

Grammar Exercises

A 空欄にあてはまる be 動詞（現在形）を入れなさい。

[例] You ＿＿＿＿＿＿ a great dancer! → You <u>are</u> a great dancer!

1. She ＿＿＿＿＿＿ very friendly.

2. I ＿＿＿＿＿＿ 19 years old.

3. ＿＿＿＿＿＿ you the owner?

4. The keys ＿＿＿＿＿＿ not on the table.

5. ＿＿＿＿＿＿ it a good company?

6. We ＿＿＿＿＿＿ ready to go.

7. My sisters ＿＿＿＿＿＿ not here.

8. No, that ＿＿＿＿＿＿ not my backpack.

9

B （　　）内の正しい語を選び、文を完成させなさい。

1. They (is / are) excited about the trip.

2. Tina and I (am / are) classmates.

3. The orange juice (is / are) in the refrigerator.

4. (Am / Are) I on time?

5. That (is / are) not Paul's bike.

C 次の文を読み、A と B のうち正しいほうを選びなさい。

1. Ted is a fast runner. Chuck is slow.

   (A) They are both fast.

   (B) Only one boy is fast.

2. The meeting time is 3:00 PM. We are ready to start. Ken is not here yet.

   (A) It is not time for the meeting.

   (B) Ken is late for the meeting.

3. Mr. Tanaka is at his office from Monday to Friday. His house is in Kobe. His office is in Osaka.

   (A) The house and the office are not in the same city.

   (B) Mr. Tanaka is in Osaka on Saturdays.

Skill Building

A **Listening**　3つの文(A, B, C)を聞き、それぞれの内容と一致しているイラストの下にその記号を書きなさい。　🎧 Track 5

1. _____　　　　　2. _____　　　　　3. _____

that's	not	I'm	is	are

Helen: Hi, Mark. Long time, no see. How ₁(   ) you?

Mark: Pretty good, thanks. How about yourself?

Helen: ₂(   ) doing well. So, do you still live downtown?

Mark: No, I'm ₃(   ) at that place anymore. I live over by the river now.

Helen: ₄(   ) a beautiful area! How ₅(   ) your wife?

Mark: She's great. Thanks for asking.

質問の答えとして最も適切なものを選びなさい。

1. (   ) What do we learn about Helen?
    A: She saw Mark last week.
    B: She doesn't live downtown anymore.
    C: She likes the area near the river.
    D: She wants to move soon.

2. (   ) Which of these is probably true?
    A: Helen knows Mark's wife.
    B: Mark and Helen work together.
    C: Few people live near the river.
    D: Mark's wife works downtown.

C **Writing**   次の 2 つの文を 1 つの文に書き換えなさい。

1. Hiroaki is tall. / Ichiro is also tall.

   Hiroaki and Ichiro _____

2. George is a singer. / He is not famous.

   George _____

3. Are you free on Saturday? / Or, are you free on Sunday?

   Are you _____

A **Reading Passage**　次の英文を読み、(　) の正しいほうの語 (句) を選びなさい。

Longyearbyen is an interesting town. ₁(It / It's) in Norway. The town is in the Arctic Circle. It (isn't / not) far from the North Pole. In fact, Longyearbyen holds a record. No other town of its size is so far north. About 2,000 people live there. ₂Many of them (is / are) miners. Others work in the tourism industry.

The small town is modern. It has an airport. There is also a movie theater, shops, and schools. Longyearbyen even has a pizza restaurant. Visitors enjoy outdoor activities and tours of the mines. But people must be careful. Longyearbyen gets very cold. In the winter, (it is / they are) often -20 °C. Also, outside of the town, there are polar bears. They are beautiful animals. ₃But they (aren't / don't) very friendly!

NOTES　　Longyearbyen「ロングイェールビーン」 Arctic Circle「北極圏」
far from ...「…から遠い」 North Pole「北極」 far north「はるか北に」
miner「鉱山労働者」 tourism industry「観光業」 polar bear「ホッキョクグマ」

B **Comprehension**　それぞれの文の内容が正しければ T(true) を、誤りであれば F(false) を○で囲みなさい。

1. Longyearbyen is near the North Pole.　　　　　　　　　　　　T　F

2. To get to Longyearbyen, people must take a boat.　　　　　　　T　F

3. For visitors to the town, the cold weather is the only danger.　　T　F

C **Translation**　前ページの英文の中で、下線が引かれている文を日本語に訳しなさい。

1. ＿＿＿＿＿＿＿＿＿＿＿＿＿＿＿＿＿＿＿＿＿＿＿＿＿＿＿＿＿＿＿＿

2. ＿＿＿＿＿＿＿＿＿＿＿＿＿＿＿＿＿＿＿＿＿＿＿＿＿＿＿＿＿＿＿＿

3. ＿＿＿＿＿＿＿＿＿＿＿＿＿＿＿＿＿＿＿＿＿＿＿＿＿＿＿＿＿＿＿＿

Reference Material

be 動詞の種類　"Be" Verb Chart

主語	現在形	過去形	現在完了
I	am	was	have been
you	are	were	have been
he	is	was	has been
she	is	was	has been
it	is	was	has been
we	are	were	have been
they	are	were	have been

There is / There are　構文

1. **There is** a fly on the table.

2. **There aren't** any people here.

3. **Are there** any apples left?

「…がある」と、なにかが存在することを表す場合には、「There ＋ be 動詞 ＋ 名詞」という構文を使う。このときの be 動詞は、直後の名詞に対応したものを使う。

2 現在形　Simple Present Tense

反復する動作や日常の習慣を表す　Repeated Actions and Habits Track 6

He **exercises** daily.

We **aren't** open on holidays.

Do you **swim** here every morning?

1. I **take** the train to school every day.
   私は毎日、列車に乗って登校します。

2. Yoshihiko **doesn't live** here anymore.
   ヨシヒコはもう、ここには住んでいません。

3. **Does** she always **eat** lunch at 12:30?
   彼女はいつも12時半に昼食をとるのですか。

毎日の通勤や通学などの反復する動作や日常の習慣などを言い表す場合には、動詞の現在形が使われる。その場合、every day、anymore、always、sometimes、rarely、never などの頻度を表す副詞とともに使われることが多い。一般動詞の否定文は、do not (don't) または does not (doesn't) を動詞の前に置き、疑問文は do または does を文頭に置いて作る。

一般的な真理や事実を述べる　Truths Track 7

There **are** five kittens in the box.

Sorry, I **don't work** here.

Can I **pay** with a credit card?

1. There **are** 24 hours in a day.
   1日は24時間ある。

2. Frank **doesn't play** the guitar.
   フランクは、（趣味として）ギターを弾かない。

3. **Does** the camera **need** four batteries?
   そのカメラには4つのバッテリーが必要ですか。

不変の自然現象や科学的な真理、日常生活の中の客観的な事実を言い表す場合に、動詞の現在形が使われる。

Track 8

The young girl really **likes** the story.

She **doesn't know** the answer.

Do you **have** a copy of the report?

1. I **feel** great!
   気分は最高！

2. The pillow **doesn't cost** very much.
   その枕は、それほど値段が高くなかった。

3. **Do** you **own** a blue car?
   あなたは青い車を持っているのですか。

> 1. feel や like、hate などの動詞で人が現在経験している感覚や感情を表現する場合、2. believe、cost、know などの動詞で現在の状態を表す場合、3. have や own などの動詞で現在なにかを「持っている」という場合に現在形が使われる。

Grammar Exercises

Ⓐ　次の文のあとに続く表現の記号を空欄に書き入れなさい。

1. Every day, I _____   (A) makes four cups.

2. The coffee machine _____   (B) watch movies here?

3. These cookies _____   (C) taste delicious!

4. Do you often _____   (D) wake up at 7:45.

Ⓑ　次の会話文の空欄に適当な語を入れなさい。

1. A: _____ you always take the bus to work?

   B: On Mondays, I ride my bike. On other days, I _____ the bus.

2. A: I love this hat. _____ it come in other sizes?

   B: No, there _____ just one size. You can adjust it in the back.

3　A: How do you _____?

   B: I feel much better, thank you.

C （　　）内に示された指示に従って、次の文を書き換えなさい。

[例]　She plays the piano every day.（疑問文に）

　　→ <u>Does she play the piano every day?</u>

1. Are there a lot of people in the club?（肯定文に）

_____

2. Gus hates waking up early.（否定文に）

_____

3. The gym is open 24 hours.（疑問文に）

_____

4. Aster doesn't work at the airport.（肯定文に）

_____

5. They have coin lockers.（否定文に）

_____

Skill Building

A **Listening**　3つの文(A, B, C)を聞き、それぞれの内容と一致しているイラストの下にその記号を書きなさい。　🎧 Track 9

1. _____　　　　2. _____　　　　3. _____

there's   have   doesn't   don't   do

Peter: Excuse me. Is Catherine here?

Staff: I'm afraid not. She ₁(   ) work here anymore.

Peter: That's too bad. I really need to talk to her. ₂(   ) you have her phone number?

Staff: I'm sorry, we ₃(   ) give out personal information. But please leave your number. I can give her the message.

Peter: Thanks so much. Do you ₄(   ) a pen?

Staff: Sure, ₅(   ) one in the cup over there.

質問の答えとして最も適切なものを選びなさい。

1. (   ) What is true about Peter?
     A: He doesn't know Catherine.
     B: He wants a cup of coffee.
     C: He works at the company.
     D: He wants to speak with Catherine.

2. (   ) What is something the staff member cannot do?
     A: Give out phone numbers   B: Let people use the phone
     C: Deliver messages   D: Talk about the company

C Writing (   ) 内の単語を並べ替え、正しい文を作りなさい。

1. My (every / father / orange juice / day / drinks).

_____

2. Madoka (like / loud / doesn't / music).

_____

3. Is (a / bakery / new / this)?

_____

Ⓐ **Reading Passage**　次の英文を読み、（　）内の正しいほうの単語を選びなさい。

₁Many people (want / wants) simple lives. But that isn't always easy. Sometimes work or school makes things challenging. Take Mayumi, for instance. She lives with her husband Takashi in Nagoya. But her company is in Tokyo. So, from Monday to Friday, she stays in Tokyo. Every weekend, she (return / returns) to Nagoya.

It's hard and tiring. ₂Mayumi (doesn't / don't) see her husband often enough. During the week, she (miss / misses) him. But it's a good job. Plus, as the saying goes, "There's light at the end of the tunnel." ₃Takashi's company (has / have) a branch in Tokyo. He may transfer there soon. Then the couple can move to Tokyo and be together every day.

NOTES　challenging「困難な、大変な」 for instance「たとえば」 tiring「疲れる」 saying「ことわざ」 go「（言葉が）…となっている」 branch「支店、支社」 transfer「転勤する」

Ⓑ **Comprehension**　それぞれの文の内容が正しければ T(true) を、誤りであれば F(false) を○で囲みなさい。

1. On Wednesdays, Mayumi is in Nagoya.　　　　　　　　　T　F

2. Mayumi and Takashi work for the same company.　　　　T　F

3. Takashi might start working in Tokyo soon.　　　　　　T　F

C **Translation**　前ページの英文の中で、下線が引かれている文を日本語に訳しなさい。

1. _____

2. _____

3. _____

——— Reference Material ———

感情や感覚を表す動詞　Verbs Expressing Feelings and Perceptions

1. This soup **tastes** great!

2. The mountain air **smells** so good.

3. How **do** you **feel**?

4. We **love** this beach.

5. I **hate** missing the start of movies.

feel(感じる)、hate(嫌う)、love(愛する)、smell(…のにおいがする)、taste(…の味がする)

現在の状態を表すとき　Other States

1. I **believe** the story.

2. I **don't want** any sugar, thank you.

3. **Do** you **know** the answer?

4. She **lives** near the university.

5. **Do** you **think** it's gold?

動詞には、一般的動作を表す「動作動詞」と、その状態をすぐには変えることのできない「状態動詞」がある。 believe（信じる）、cost（要する）、know（知っている）、think（考える）、want（ほしい）、live（生活している）などの状態動詞は、現在のことを述べるときには現在形のまま使われ、進行形にすることはできない。

3 過去形 Simple Past Tense

 Track 10

He **ate** a big breakfast.

There **were** some pretty balloons.

I **did not close** the door.

1. I **called** Bruce this morning.
   今朝、ブルースに電話をしました。

2. The friends **were** happy to see each other.
   その友人らは、会えてうれしかった。

3. Mr. Jimenez **did not leave** a message.
   ヒメネスさんは伝言を残さなかった。

> 動詞の過去形は、過去のある時点における動作や状態、過去の習慣などを表すために使われる。 be
> 動詞の過去形は was と were の２種類だが、一般動詞は動詞の原形に -ed を付けるもの（規則動詞）
> と、独自の形を持ったもの（不規則動詞）とがある。否定文を作るときは、be 動詞では was not
> (wasn't) か were not (weren't) を使い、一般動詞では、「did not (didn't) ＋動詞の原形」となる。

過去形の疑問文　Asking Questions Track 11

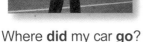
Where **did** my car **go**?

Did you **enjoy** your meal?

What **did** Marco **say**?

1. **Did** you **turn** the light off? (Yes, I **did**.)
   灯りは消しましたか。（はい、消しました。）

2. When **did** he **leave**? (He **left** at 10:00.)
   彼はいつ帰ったのですか。（彼は10時に帰りました。）

3. Where **did** Nancy **go**? (I don't know. Maybe she **went** home.)
   ナンシーはどこに行ったのですか。（わかりません。たぶん、家に帰ったのでしょう。）

> 過去形の疑問文は、be 動詞の場合は was か were を文頭に置いて作り、一般動詞の場合は did を
> 文頭に置いて「Did ＋主語＋動詞の原形」のようにして作る。疑問詞を使った疑問文では、「疑問
> 詞＋ did ＋主語＋動詞の原形」という形になる。

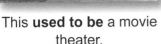

This **used to be** a movie theater.

I **used to work** at that pizza restaurant.

She **didn't use to wear** hats. Now she always does.

1. We **used to live** in Aomori. Now we live in Fukuoka.

   私たちは昔、青森に住んでいました。今は、福岡に住んでいます。

2. That **used to be** a parking lot. Now there's a clinic there.

   そこは以前、駐車場でした。今、そこには診療所があります。

3. I **didn't use to like** jazz. But now I love it!

   前はジャズが好きではありませんでした。でも、今は大好きです。

> 過去の長い期間にわたる習慣について「昔はよく…していた」と言ったり、過去において長期間続いていた状態について「以前は…だったものだ」と説明したりする場合に、「used to ＋動詞の原形」が使われる。否定文は「didn't use to ＋動詞の原形」。

Grammar Exercises

A （　　）内の動詞を過去形に変えなさい。

[例] We _____ to him yesterday. (talk)

→ We <u>talked</u> to him yesterday.

1. She _____ a bracelet and a pendant. (buy)

2. I _____ not at my office this morning. (be)

3. You _____ a beautiful garden. (plant)

4. The friends _____ a bus to Yokohama. (take)

5. Mark and Francis _____ not at the wedding. (be)

6. I _____ to high school there. (go)

7. Jack _____ his guests into his home. (welcome)

8. Everyone _____ carefully to the speech. (listen)

21

B 次の質問に対応する正しい返事を選びなさい。

1. _____ Did they pick up the package?

2. _____ What did she say?

3. _____ Were the shirts the right size?

4. _____ Where did you go?

(A) No, they weren't.

(B) We went to the beach.

(C) She said she may be late.

(D) Yes, they did.

C 次の文を読み、ＡとＢのうち内容が正しいほうを選びなさい。

1. John lived in Kamakura from 2007 to 2010. In 2010, he moved to Hiroshima. He still lives there.
   (A) John used to live in Kamakura.
   (B) John lived in Kamakura in 2011.

2. Toru and Tina went to Phone World. Everything was too expensive. They decided to look for a phone online.
   (A) They bought a phone at Phone World.
   (B) They didn't buy anything at Phone World.

3. After university, Hideki got a job at a law firm. Eri joined the firm two years later. One year after that, Hideki changed jobs.
   (A) Hideki and Eri were classmates.
   (B) Hideki and Eri were co-workers.

Skill Building

A **Listening** 4つの文(A, B, C, D)を聞き、それぞれの内容と一致しているイラストの下にその記号を書きなさい。 🎧 Track 13

1. _____   2. _____   3. _____   4. _____

B Speaking 　次の会話文を読み、以下のリストから適切な語 (句) を選んで空欄を埋めなさい。

| bought | played | did | used | didn't |

Toshi: 　Hi, Lana. ₁(　　　　) you have a nice time in Hakone?

Lana: 　Yes, thank you. We went to a beautiful museum. We also

　　　　₂(　　　　) in the snow. I even built a snowman!

Toshi: 　Sounds fun, but kind of cold.

Lana: 　I ₃(　　　) to live in Hokkaido. So I love the snow. Anyway,

　　　　sorry I ₄(　　　) take many photos. But I ₅(　　　) you a

　　　　present.

Toshi: 　Wow, it's a little snow globe. Thank you!

Lana: 　You're welcome.

質問の答えとして最も適切なものを選びなさい。

1. (　) What does Lana say about Hokkaido?
　　　　A: She once lived there.
　　　　B: She loves snow globes from Hokkaido.
　　　　C: She just took a trip there.
　　　　D: She doesn't like the snowy weather.

2. (　) What is something that Lana did not do in Hakone?
　　　　A: Buy a present　　　　　B: Take a lot of photos
　　　　C: Build a snowman　　　　D: Visit a museum

C Writing 　次の質問に対し、(　) 内に示した単語を使って過去形で答えなさい。

1. Hey, Ann. What did you do last night? (go, a birthday party)

　I _____

2. Did Jane talk to Martin? (talk, him)

　No, she _____

3. Where did they work in Nagano? (used to, a bookstore)

　They _____

A **Reading Passage**　次の文章の空欄に、[　]内の動詞を過去形に変えて入れなさい。

The history of communication says a lot about us. Two hundred years ago, people loved to write letters to each other. ₁Back then, letters _____ [be] often long and detailed. In 1838, the world saw an important new invention: the telegraph. The system was fast. But it _____ [have] limits.

₂In 1876, the telephone _____ [make] voice chats possible. The invention changed the world. But for 100 years, talking long distance _____ [be] not cheap. Everything changed in 1994 with a new tool: the Internet. E-mails (and later voice chats) were free and easy.

₃Over time, websites like Facebook and Twitter _____ [become] very popular. People wrote billions of short messages to each other. Cell phone users also fell in love with text messaging. So these days, we can talk or write to anyone, anytime. But we choose many short messages over a few long ones.

NOTES　detailed「詳しい、具体的な」 invention「発明（品）」 telegraph「電報」 limits「限界」 chat「おしゃべり」 Facebook「インターネットを通じ、参加者が実名で交流を図るオンラインサービス」 Twitter「短い文を投稿したり読んだりできるインターネット上の情報サービス」 cell phone「携帯電話」 text messaging「携帯メール」

B **Comprehension**　それぞれの文の内容が正しければ T(true) を、誤りであれば F(false) を○で囲みなさい。

1. In the mid-19th century, sending telegraphs was quick.　　　T　F

2. For a century, long-distance phone calls were expensive.　　　T　F

3. Facebook users prefer long messages.　　　T　F

C **Translation**　前ページの英文の中で、下線が引かれている文を日本語に訳しなさい。

1. _____

2. _____

3. _____

--- **Reference Material** ---

規則動詞の過去形の作り方　List of Past Tense Spelling Rules

1) ほとんどの動詞は、原形の語尾に ed を付ける。

例：talk – talked / repair – repaired / pick – picked

2) 語尾が「子音＋ y」の動詞は、y を i に変えて ed を付ける。

例：try – tried / rely – relied / marry – married

3) 語尾が e で終わる動詞は、d だけを付ける。

例：love – loved / smile – smiled / prepare – prepared

4) 語尾が c で終わる動詞は、ked を付ける。

例：panic – panicked / mimic – mimicked / picnic – picnicked

5) 語尾が「子音＋母音＋子音」の動詞の場合：

・動詞の音節が１つだけならば、最後の子音を重ねて ed を付ける。

例：flip – flipped / mop – mopped / bar – barred

（ただし、語尾の子音が h、w、x の場合はそのまま ed を付ける）

・動詞に音節が２つあり、最後の音節にアクセントがあるときは、最後の子音を重ねて ed を付ける。

例：submit – submitted / refer – referred / remit – remitted

（ただし、最後の音節にアクセントがない場合は、ただ ed を付ければよい。）

例：offer – offered / listen – listened

4 代名詞 Pronouns

主語として使う代名詞　Subject Pronouns Track 14

I work at a bank.

She doesn't live around here.

Did **he** walk home?

1. **He** works at a bakery.
   彼はパン屋で働いています。

2. **We** don't like spicy food.
   私たちは辛い食べ物は好きではありません。

3. Do **you** have any brothers or sisters?
   あなたには兄弟か姉妹がいますか。

> 人や物を表す代名詞は、動作の主体、すなわち主語として使うことができる。語順は基本的に「主語＋動詞（＋目的語・補語）」となる。疑問文の場合は、do、does、did などの助動詞を先頭に置いて「助動詞＋代名詞＋動詞（＋目的語・補語）」とする。

目的語として使う代名詞　Object Pronouns Track 15

Joe gave **her** flowers.

I didn't meet **him** in Italy.

Did Mom buy **it** online?

1. Jennifer sent **me** a card.
   ジェニファーは私にカードを送ってきた。

2. I did not see **her** at the office.
   私は彼女を会社で見かけなかった。

3. Should we ask **them** to come?
   私たちは彼らに来るように頼むべきですか。

> 代名詞を動詞の目的語として使う場合は、その直後に置かれる。ただし、人を表す人称代名詞の場合には、you 以外は次のように語形が変化する：I – me / we – us / he – him / she – her / they – them

Track 16

The dog is **ours**.

That isn't **our** car.

Is this coat **yours**?

1. The wallet is **mine**.
   その財布は私のものです。

2. That isn't **their** logo.
   それは彼らのロゴではありません。

3. What's **your** address?
   あなたのご住所はどちらですか。

> 代名詞を使って「の…」という所有関係を表す場合は、「代名詞の所有格＋もの」という形をとる。また、it 以外の代名詞には、mine（私のもの）、yours（あなたのもの）というように、それだけで名詞の働きをする独立所有格（→ p.31）がある。

Grammar Exercises

A 次の文には、代名詞が誤って使われている箇所があります。その代名詞に線を引き、正しいものを空欄に書きなさい。

[例] I am Chika. Here is me name card.

→ I am Chika. Here is ~~me~~ name card.   <u> my </u>

1. My name is Jack. My am from England.   <u>   </u>

2. There are so many bicycles here. Oh, that one is my.   <u>   </u>

3. Hi, Taro. It's so nice to see your!   <u>   </u>

4. I can't reach the salt. Can you please hand it to I?   <u>   </u>

5. These pants are great. Do them come in grey?   <u>   </u>

6. Where is him house? Isn't it in this area?   <u>   </u>

7. My dad bought I some nice gloves.   <u>   </u>

B （　）内の正しい語を選び、文を完成させなさい。

1. (He / Him) is my good friend.

2. Please give (she / her) my best wishes.

3. It's getting late. Stan and (I / me) need to wake up early tomorrow.

4. Do you want to see (my / mine) new purse?

5. I saw Theo today. I heard the news from (he / him).

6. These are really nice paintings. Were (they / them) done by a local artist?

7. Is this pen mine or (your / yours)?

8. The car isn't (their / theirs). They drive a Toyota.

C 空欄にあてはまる代名詞を入れなさい。

1. A: Is this your watch?

   B: No, it isn't. Maybe it's Anthony's. You should show it to _____.

2. A: I need to talk to Linda.

   B: I saw her a few minutes ago. _____ is in the library.

3. A: My phone is broken. Can I borrow _____?

   B: Of course. Here you are.

Skill Building

A Listening　3つの文(A, B, C)を聞き、それぞれの内容と一致しているイラストの下にその記号を書きなさい。　🎧 Track 17

1. _____

2. _____

3. _____

B **Speaking**　次の会話文を読み、以下のリストから適切な単語を選んで空欄を埋めなさい。

you	his	it	he	him

Thomas:　We got a new salesperson today. He seems like a nice guy.

Wendy:　That's good. Where is ₁(   ) from?

Thomas:　Dallas, I think. I showed ₂(   ) around the office. He really liked the employee break room.

Wendy:　₃(   ) really is a pretty room. I love the sofa in there. So, are ₄(   ) two on the same floor?

Thomas:　Actually, ₅(   ) desk is right next to mine.

Wendy:　Nice. He sounds like a good guy to work with.

質問の答えとして最も適切なものを選びなさい。

1. (   ) Which of these is true?
　　A: Thomas recently took a business trip.
　　B: Wendy has a new desk.
　　C: Thomas likes his new co-worker.
　　D: Wendy is from Dallas.

2. (   ) Which room does Wendy like a lot?
　　A: The break room   B: The salesperson's office
　　C: The cafeteria   D: The meeting room

C **Writing**　(   ) 内の単語を並べ替え、正しい文を作りなさい。

1. We (details / them / the / gave).

_____

2. The (mine / not / notebook / is / black).

_____

3. Can (tell / station's name / me / the / you)?

_____

A **Reading Passage**　次の英文を読み、（　）内の正しいほうの単語を選びなさい。

Kenji just graduated from university. ₁(He / Him) has big plans. The young man wants to start his own business. Kenji loves graphic design. (It / He) was his favorite class in university. Now he wants to start a web design company. It will be hard work, but he wants to give it a try. He has a few ideas on how to get started.

Masao, one of (his / he) classmates, is an excellent designer. He might join Kenji's company. Another classmate, Hiroko, studied marketing. ₂Kenji got some good advice from (she / her). She said, "There are many great companies out there. ₃But you have to tell people about (you / your) company. That's why marketing is so important." Her other "keys to success" are great service and hard work.

NOTES　graduate from ... 「…を卒業する」　business「会社」　excellent「優秀な」
out there「世の中には」　hard work「勤勉さ」

B **Comprehension**　それぞれの文の内容が正しければ T(true) を、誤りであれば F(false) を○で囲みなさい。

1. In university, Kenji enjoyed studying business the most.　　　　T　F

2. Hiroko knows a lot about marketing.　　　　T　F

3. Kenji has some money to spend. Hiroko would likely suggest spending it all on office furniture.　　　　T　F

C **Translation**　前ページの英文の中で、下線が引かれている文を日本語に訳しなさい。

1. _____

2. _____

3. _____

Reference Material

指示代名詞　Demonstrative Pronouns

1. **That** is a great name for a band!

2. I don't want **those**.

3. Are **these** your keys?

自分の近くにあるもの、身近に感じられるものは this「これ」（複数は these「これら」）、それよりも遠くにあるものについては that「あれ」（複数は those「あれら」）という代名詞を使う。

再帰代名詞　Reflexive Pronouns

1. She bought **herself** a new dress.

2. He didn't do it all **himself**.

3. I built the bookcase by **myself**.

再帰代名詞は、目的語として「自分を…する」という意味で使われるほか、動作をする人を強調したいときに使われる。また、by + ... self で、「自分1人で、独力で」という意味を表す。

代名詞一覧表　Chart of Pronoun Types

主格	目的格	所有格	独立所有格	再帰代名詞
I	me	my	mine	myself
you	you	your	yours	yourself / yourselves
he	him	his	his	himself
she	her	her	hers	herself
it	it	its	-	itself
we	us	our	ours	ourselves
they	them	their	theirs	themselves

5 前置詞　Prepositions

時を表す前置詞　Time Track 18

The concert starts **at** 7:30.

It doesn't snow **in** July.

Was it busy **on** Christmas?

1. My cousin was born **in** 1988.
   わたしのいとこは1988年生まれです。

2. The exhibit doesn't open **until** March 10.
   その展覧会が開催されるのは3月10日からだ。

3. Will you arrive **at** 3:00 or 4:00?
   あなたが到着するのは3時、それとも4時？

> 英語には、時を表すための前置詞がいくつかあり、その使い分けを覚えておく必要がある。一般的な規則として、「…時に」では at、「…日に／…曜日に」では on、「…月に／…年に／春（夏・秋・冬）に」では in が使われる。after と since はどちらも「…のあとで」という意味だが、since は現時点まで「…からずっと」という継続の意味が含まれている。また、by と until も「…まで」という意味だが、by には期限、until には「…までずっと」という継続の意味が含まれている。

場所を表す前置詞　Location Track 19

The boat is **under** the bridge.

The bag is **on** the floor.

The chair is **beside** the table.

1. I will hang the calendar **beside** the window.
   そのカレンダーは窓の横にかけることにします。

2. There aren't any Indian restaurants **near** here.
   この近くにはインド料理店が1軒もありません。

3. Is your car **in front of** the convenience store?
   あなたの車はコンビニの正面に止めてありますか。

> 場所を表す前置詞でよく使われるのが at、in、on で、at は具体的な建物や「…番地」など、広がりのない狭い場所、in は市町村や区、県、地域、国などの広い場所、on は「…通り」などに使われることが多い。これ以外の前置詞についても、使い分けを整理して覚えておくとよい。

Track 20

My co-worker is **against** the idea.

Put the thread **through** the needle, like this.

Did you walk **over** the little bridge?

1. The flowers are **for** my mother.
   その花は母にあげるものです。

2. I never go outside **without** my umbrella.
   私は外出するときは必ず傘を持っていきます。

3. Are you still **against** the plan?
   あなたは今でもその計画に反対ですか。

前置詞は、時間や場所以外にもさまざまな意味を表すことができる。例文中の for は「…のために」、without は「…なしで」、against は「…に反対で」ということである。2 の「never do without A 」は、「A なしでは決して〜しない＝〜するときは必ず A を手放さない」という慣用表現。

Grammar Exercises

Ⓐ　正しい前置詞を選んで、文を完成させなさい。

1. I will go to Sapporo (at / in) May.

2. They can park (in / on) front of the house.

3. The ball went (over / across) the fence.

4. We can't leave yet. We have to stay (by / until) 6:00.

5. Do you see the sign (by / up) the door? It says "No pets."

6. I love talking (between / with) Nate. He's a very interesting person.

7. I need some coffee. Otherwise, I might fall asleep (around / during) the movie.

8. Ms. Sato is (through / against) the investment. She thinks it's too risky.

B 次の文のあとに続く表現の記号を空欄に書き入れなさい。

1. I have karate class _____   (A) near the train station?

2. The present is _____   (B) to Saturday.

3. Is there a bookstore _____   (C) at 4:30 PM.

4. We are open from Monday _____   (D) about this file?

5. Can I ask you _____   (E) for my sister.

C 次の文を読み、A と B のうち正しいほうを選びなさい。

1. She has class from 2:00 to 3:45.
   (A) The class is over at 2:00.
   (B) The class lasts until 3:45.

2. My bank is on 4th Street. Further down the street, there is a grocery store. Even further down the street, there is a high school.
   (A) The school is next to the bank.
   (B) The store is on 4th Street. It is in between a bank and a school.

3. Chris wants to move to Okayama. Dana agrees with him.
   (A) Dana is for the idea.
   (B) Dana is against the idea.

Skill Building

A **Listening** 3つの文(A, B, C)を聞き、それぞれの内容と一致しているイラストの下にその記号を書きなさい。　🎧 Track 21

1. _____   2. _____   3. _____

B **Speaking** 次の会話文を読み、以下のリストから適切な単語を選んで空欄を埋めなさい。

| on | until | by | in | to |

Sue: Thanks for helping me. I couldn't do all this ₁(   ) myself.

Frank: My pleasure. Where do these boxes of copy paper go?

Sue: Those go ₂(   ) the other room. Please put them next ₃(   ) the copy machine.

Frank: Sure. So, when is the store's grand opening?

Sue: Actually, it's ₄(   ) June 15.

Frank: That's pretty soon! Well, I can stay ₅(   ) 7:30 tonight. If you want, I can come back again tomorrow.

質問の答えとして最も適切なものを選びなさい。

1. (   ) What do we learn about the store?
     A: Yesterday was its first day.
     B: It's an office supply shop.
     C: Sue and Frank own the store.
     D: It has more than one room.

2. (   ) What does Frank offer to do?
     A: Make some copies   B: Help Sue another day
     C: Buy dinner at 7:30   D: Clean the store

C **Writing** 次の２つの文を、（   ）内の語句を使って１つの文にしなさい。

1. They open at 11:00 AM. / They close at 8:00 PM. (from, to)

     They are _____

2. I do not agree with the suggestion. / Martha doesn't agree either. (against)

     We are both _____

3. To the left of the clinic is a church. / To the right is a pharmacy. (in between)

     The clinic is _____

Ⓐ **Reading Passage**　次の英文を読み、（　　）内の正しいほうの単語を選びなさい。

Disney World is a magical place. The park is (in / at) Orlando, Florida. ₁<u>It first opened (on / in) 1971.</u> It's a place loved (by / for) children and adults. People enjoy the rides, shows, and parades. They also enjoy seeing Mickey, Donald, and other characters. Plus, visitors love buying toys and other souvenirs.

₂<u>The park opens (at / to) 8:00 or 9:00 AM.</u> It usually closes at around 10:00 PM. Every year, Disney World gets more than 15 million visitors. Some fans love the park so much that they travel there several times per year. ₃<u>Visitors come (from / to) all over the world.</u> California, Japan, France, and Hong Kong also have Disney parks. But Disney World is the biggest of them all.

NOTES　　**magical**「魔法のような、魅力的な」 **adult**「大人」 **ride**「乗り物」
of course「もちろん」 **more than ...**「…以上の」 **million**「百万」

Ⓑ **Comprehension**　それぞれの文の内容が正しければ T(true) を、誤りであれば F(false) を◯で囲みなさい。

1. Disney World first opened more than 50 years ago. 　　　T　F

2. Disney World is usually closed at 9:00 PM. 　　　T　F

3. Hong Kong Disney is the same size as Disney World. 　　　T　F

Ⓒ Translation　前ページの英文の中で、下線が引かれている文を日本語に訳しなさい。

1. _____

2. _____

3. _____

─── Reference Material ───

時を表す前置詞　List of Time Prepositions

after（…のあとで）、at（…［のとき・時］に）、before（…の前に）、between（…の間に）、by（…までに）、during（…の間に）、for（…の期間）、from（…から）、in（…［月・季節・年・世紀］に／…以内に）、on（…［曜日・日］に）、since（…以来）、throughout（…の間じゅう）、to（…まで）、until（…までずっと）

場所を表す前置詞　List of Location Prepositions

above（…の上方に）、across（…の向こう側に）、along（…に沿って）、around（…の周囲に／…を曲がったところに）、behind（…の背後に）、below（…の下方に）、beneath（…の真下に）、beside（…のわきに）、(in) between（…の間に）、by（…のすぐそばに）、down（…の下に）、in（…の中に）、in front of（…の正面に）、inside（…の内部に）、into（…の中へ）、near（…の近くに）、on（…の上に）、onto（…の上へ）、outside（…の外に）、over（…の真上に）、throughout（…のすみずみに）、under（…の下に）、up（…の上のほうに）、upon（…の上に）

その他の前置詞　List of Other Prepositions

about（…について）、against（…に反して）、by（…によって）、for（…のために）、of（…の）、over（…をめぐって）、through（…によって）、to（…に対して）、toward(s)（…に向かって）、with（…とともに／…を使って）、without（…なしに）

6 進行形 **Progressive Tenses**

現在進行形　Present Progressive Track 22

They **are building** a house.

She **is walking** her dog.

We **are not doing** anything today.

1. I **am having** a lot of fun.
   私は大いに楽しんでいます。

2. She**'s hoping** to find a part-time job.
   彼女はアルバイトを見つけたいと思っている。

3. My parents **are not using** the car today.
   私の両親は、今日は車を使っていない。

> ある動作や状態が今現在も続いている場合、「be 動詞＋動詞の ing 形」を使って「今…している」という意味を表すことができる。その場合、be 動詞は主語と対応した形（am / are / is）を使う。否定文にする場合は、be 動詞のあとに not を置く。

過去進行形　Past Progressive Track 23

We **were sitting** under a tree.

The friends **were jogging** together.

Sean **was not playing** his guitar.

1. I **was living** in Nagasaki in 2016.
   私は2016年当時、長崎に住んでいた。

2. My mom **wasn't planning** to get a new car.
   私の母は新車を買うつもりはなかった。

3. They **were thinking** of traveling to France.
   彼らはフランスに旅行しようと考えていた。

> 過去のある時点において進行中だった動作や状態を表す場合は、「be 動詞の過去形＋動詞の ing 形」を使って「…していた」と表現することができる。この場合の be 動詞は、was もしくは were のいずれかである。否定文にする場合は、be 動詞のあとに not を置く。

Are you **leaving**?　　What **are** you **cooking**?　　**Were** they **using** the boat?

1. **Are** you still **taking** photography classes?
   あなたは今も写真教室に参加しているのですか。

2. **Were** you **working** in the garden all morning?
   あなたは午前中ずっと庭仕事をしていたのですか。

3. **Was** Carl **trying** to contact me yesterday?
   カールは昨日、私に連絡を取ろうとしていたのですか。

> 現在形でも過去形でも、進行形の疑問文を作る場合は「be 動詞＋主語＋動詞」の語順となる。また、What や Where などの疑問詞で始まる疑問文は、さらにその疑問詞を文頭に置く。

Grammar Exercises

Ⓐ　（　　）内の指示に従って、次の文を書き換えなさい。

[例] I was resting. （現在進行形に）　→　<u>I am resting.</u>

1. They cleaned their rooms. （過去進行形に）

   _____

2. We are watching TV. （否定文に）

   _____

3. Where do you live now? （現在進行形に）

   _____

4. He studies psychology. （現在進行形に）

   _____

5. We are trying our best. （過去進行形に）

   _____

B （　）内に示された動詞と時制を使って、進行形の文を作りなさい。

[例] We _____ _____.（study・現在）→ We are studying.

1. She _____ _____.（sleep・現在）

2. All of my friends _____ _____.（dance・過去）

3. Bob and Kate _____ _____ _____.（play・過去＋否定）

4. One of us _____ _____.（go・現在）

5. What _____ you _____?（do・過去）

C 次の会話文の空欄に適当な語を入れなさい。

1. A: Hi, Rudolfo. Where (　　　　　) you (　　　　　)?
   B: Hey, Emily. I'm going to the supermarket.

2. A: Are you still helping Aaron?
   B: Yes, I (　　　　　) (　　　　　) him study for the test.

3. A: Kim looked sick yesterday morning. Was she feeling all right?
   B: No, she (　　　　　) (　　　　　) (　　　　　) well. She went
      to the clinic in the afternoon.

--- **Skill Building** ---

A **Listening** 3つの文(A, B, C)を聞き、それぞれの内容と一致しているイラストの
下にその記号を書きなさい。 🎧 Track 25

1. _____   2. _____   3. _____

| are | is | am | were | was |

Mitsuko:　Sorry I couldn't see you yesterday. I was in Sapporo all day.

Hiro:　　　That's all right. What ₁(　　　　　) you doing there?

Mitsuko:　I ₂(　　　　　) visiting my uncle in the hospital.

Hiro:　　　I'm sorry to hear that. Is it serious?

Mitsuko:　No, he just had a skiing accident. He ₃(　　　　　) getting
　　　　　better now. Also, my mother and sister ₄(　　　　　) taking
　　　　　turns making his meals. They visit him every day.

Hiro:　　　That's so nice of them! Actually, I ₅(　　　　　) hoping to visit
　　　　　Sapporo soon. Maybe we can go together.

質問の答えとして最も適切なものを選びなさい。

1. (　　) Who went skiing in Sapporo?
　　A: Hiro　　　　　　　　　　B: Mitsuko
　　C: Hiro's sister　　　　　　D: Mitsuko's uncle

2. (　　) What does Hiro suggest doing?
　　A: Going skiing with some friends
　　B: Traveling to Sapporo with Mitsuko
　　C: Visiting a classmate in the hospital
　　D: Making a meal for a relative

C Writing　(　　) 内の単語を並べ替え、正しい文を作りなさい。

1. She (home / driving / is / now).

_____

2. The model (wearing / not / jewelry / was).

_____

3. Are (for / joining / they / dinner / us)?

_____

A Reading Passage [ ]内の動詞を進行形に変えて、それぞれの空欄に入れなさい。

In many countries, people love Japanese comics, cartoons, and toys. Pop culture items are sold at stores and online. ₁Thanks to pop culture, many Japanese terms (_____) (_____) [enter] the English language. ₂People (_____) (_____) [use] words like "manga" and "anime" in daily life. In fact, for more than half a century, many of the world's most famous cartoons and characters have come from Japan.

Some overseas fans watch anime in Japanese. The shows often have English subtitles on the bottom. Other people prefer listening to English versions of the shows. For manga, most fans read English translations. A few prefer the original versions. It's a fun way to learn Japanese. ₃One thing is certain: Japanese pop culture (_____) (_____) [become] very popular!

NOTES comic「漫画本」 cartoon「アニメ」 pop culture「大衆文化」 item「商品」
term「ことば」 daily「毎日の」 show「番組」 subtitle「字幕」 translation「翻訳」
certain「明らかな」

B Comprehension それぞれの文の内容が正しければ T(true) を、誤りであれば F(false) を○で囲みなさい。

1. The article does not mention buying items from friends.   T   F

2. The word "anime" is used outside of Japan.   T   F

3. Manga is always read in Japanese.   T   F

1. _____

2. _____

3. _____

— **Reference Material** —

動詞の -ing 形の作り方　Chart of Progressive Form Spelling Rules

動詞の種類	規則	例	
一般的な動詞	-ing を付ける	lift attend	lifting attending
語尾が発音しない e で終わる動詞	e を除いて -ing を付ける	make drive	making driving
語尾が ie で終わる動詞	ie を除いて -ying を付ける	tie lie	tying lying
語尾が「子音＋強調される母音＋子音」で終わる動詞	最後の1文字を追加してから -ing を付ける	run submit	running submitting
語尾が「子音＋強調されない母音＋子音」で終わる動詞	-ing を付ける	visit limit	visiting limiting
語尾が w、x、y で終わる動詞	-ing を付ける	fix try	fixing trying

1. My son **is attending** a small kindergarten.

2. For the group lunch, **are** you **making** an appetizer or a dessert?

3. Let's try to be quiet. Dad **is lying down** in his bedroom.

4. **Are** you **planning** to buy a new washing machine?

5. The store **is limiting** purchases to one per person.

6. Sorry, I didn't hear you. I **was sawing up** some firewood.

数えられる名詞　Countable Nouns

Track 26

The **trees** are tall.　　My **cat** doesn't like getting wet.　　Do you have any **coins**?

1. The **store** sells many interesting **things**.
   その店は、おもしろいものをいろいろ売っている。

2. **Cities** are not usually quiet **places**.
   都会は、たいてい静かなところではない。

3. Can you carry all the **bags**?
   そのカバンをすべて運ぶことができますか。

> 「建物」や「場所」、「品物」など、具体的な形や範囲がある名詞は、数えられる名詞（可算名詞）として扱われ、それが複数ある場合にはふつう語尾に s が付けられる。英語の辞書では countable の頭文字「C」で示される。

数えられない名詞　Uncountable Nouns

Track 27

Would you like some **water**?　　He doesn't take **sugar** with his coffee.　　How can we get around this **traffic**?

1. Here is the **information**.
   ここにその情報があります。

2. The accountant doesn't have enough **time**.
   その会計士には十分な時間がない。

3. Did you buy some **milk**?
   牛乳は買いましたか。

> 「情報」や「時間」、「液体」など、まとまった形やはっきりした範囲を持たない名詞は、数えられない名詞（不可算名詞）で、複数形にすることはできない。辞書では uncountable の頭文字「U」で表される。

The Eiffel Tower is famous.

Would you like to see **a** photo of Luke?

Here is **the** contract you wanted to review.

1. It's **a** big university. **The** university has a lot of great teachers.
   そこは大きな大学です。その大学には多くの優れた教員がいます。

2. **The** Yellow River is not in Italy.
   イエロー・リバーがあるのはイタリアではない。

3. Is that **a** rare coin? **The** coin looks really old.
   それは珍しいコインですか。そのコインはずいぶん昔のものに見えます。

> 不定冠詞の a や an は、1つのまとまった形のある名詞の前に付けられる。ただし、同じ名詞に再び言及するときは、定冠詞の the を付けて「その…」と表現する。状況から特定できるものには最初から the を付ける。また、特定の川、山、海、海峡、群島、砂漠などの地名や船、建物などの固有名詞の一部、「月」や「太陽」など自然界に1つしかない天体名の前には the が付けられる。

Grammar Exercises

A （　）内の正しい語を選び、文を完成させなさい。

1. It was (a / an / the) great game. Even better, our team won!

2. Please turn down (a / an / the) music. It's too loud.

3. A few (house / houses) in the neighborhood are 100 years old.

4. We have (space / spaces) in the back. You can put your things there.

5. Do you have (a / an / the) extra jacket? It's kind of cold outside.

6. This is the living room. Let me show you (a / an / the) kitchen.

7. I don't have any (money / moneys). I spent it all.

8. We played four (game / games) of Go. He won three of them.

B （　）内の名詞を正しい形に変えて空欄に入れなさい。

[例]　a lot of _____ (egg) → a lot of <u>eggs</u>

1. some _____ (luck)

2. many _____ (singer)

3. a few _____ (child)

4. very little _____ (ice)

5. three _____ (bus)

C （　）内に a, an または the を入れなさい。

1. A: Oakdale is (　　　　) small town. It's about 75 kilometers from here. We drove around (　　　　) town yesterday. There are pretty oak trees along (　　　　) main road.

   B: It sounds like (　　　　) beautiful place.

2. A: How does (　　　　) weather look today?

   B: I just checked my phone. There's good and bad news. There may be (　　　　) rainstorm in the morning. But (　　　　) weather should clear up by (　　　　) afternoon.

Skill Building

A **Listening**　4つの文(A, B, C, D)を聞き、それぞれの内容と一致しているイラストの下にその記号を書きなさい。　🎧 Track 29

1. _____　　　2. _____　　　3. _____　　　4. _____

the	person	an	people	a

Server:　Welcome to the Gardener. How many ₁(　　　　　) are in your party?

Guest:　Six for now. But one more ₂(　　　　　) might join us later.

Server:　No problem. Would you like ₃(　　　　　) table in the smoking or non-smoking section?

Guest:　Non-smoking, please.

Server:　Certainly, right this way. The salad bar is at ₄(　　　　　) back of the restaurant. Here's ₅(　　　　　) extra menu for your friend.

Guest:　Perfect, thank you.

質問の答えとして最も適切なものを選びなさい。

1. (　　) If the other friend comes, how many people will eat together?
　　　A: Four　　　　　　　　B: Five
　　　C: Six　　　　　　　　D: Seven

2. (　　) What does the guest ask for?
　　　A: A seat at the back of the restaurant
　　　B: An extra bowl for the salad bar
　　　C: A table in the non-smoking section
　　　D: A birthday cake for their party

1. My watch is broken. (need, new watch)

　I _____

2. Tom is my best friend. (work, gas station)

　He _____

3. Yesterday, we bought a new computer. (machine, very fast)

　I think _____

A **Reading Passage**　次の英文を読み、（　）内の正しいほうの単語を選びなさい。

₁<u>Cambridge University is (a / the) famous school.</u> (A / The) university was founded more than 800 years ago. Many well-known people have gone to school there. They include Alfred Tennyson, Charles Darwin, and James Watson. Cambridge has also attracted famous teachers like Isaac Newton and Stephen Hawking. ₂<u>They do important (research / researches) at the school.</u>

₃<u>Cambridge is also (a / the) publishing center.</u> Cambridge University Press is the oldest publisher in the world. They started publishing books in 1584. Since then, they have published new books every single year! Their catalogue includes books on history, science, and many other (subject / subjects).

NOTES　found「設立する」 well-known「有名な」 Alfred Tennyson「アルフレッド・テニスン（イギリスの詩人）」 Charles Darwin「チャールズ・ダーウィン（イギリスの博物学者）」 James Watson「ジェイムズ・ワトソン（アメリカの生物学者）」 attract「引き寄せる」 Isaac Newton「アイザック・ニュートン（イギリスの天文学者）」 Stephen Hawking「スティーブン・ホーキング（イギリスの天体物理学者）」 publishing「出版活動（の）」 publisher「出版社」

B **Comprehension**　それぞれの文の内容が正しければ T(true) を、誤りであれば F(false) を○で囲みなさい。

1. Cambridge University is more than 800 years old.　　T　F

2. James Watson was one of Cambridge's famous teachers.　　T　F

3. Cambridge University Press still publishes books.　　T　F

C **Translation** 前ページの英文の中で、下線が引かれている文を日本語に訳しなさい。

1. _____

2. _____

3. _____

Reference Material

[不可算名詞の種類　List of Common Uncountable Nouns]

物質名詞：	copper（銅）、steel（鉄鋼）、milk（ミルク）、gasoline（ガソリン）、paper（紙）、tea（お茶）、gold（金）、silver（銀）など
抽象名詞：	advice（忠告）、faith（信頼）、happiness（幸福）、sadness（悲しみ）、information（情報）、luck（幸運）、music（音楽）、news（ニュース）、time（時間）など
集合名詞：	baggage（手荷物）、data（データ）、furniture（家具）、clothing（衣類）、machinery（機械類）、staff（人員）など

[不可算名詞の量を表現するための語句　Measure Words for Uncountable Nouns]

量の大小を表す：	a great deal of（大量の）、a little（少量の）、little（ほとんどない）、a lot of (lots of)（たくさんの）、any（いくらかの）、some（いくらかの）、much（たくさんの）、plenty of（大量の）など
単位や形 + of ...：	bottle(s) of（ボトル…本の）、bucket(s) of（バケツ…杯の）、cup(s) of（カップ…杯の）、gallon(s) of（…ガロンの）、liter(s) of（…リットルの）、lump(s) of（…個の）、slice(s) of（…切れの）、piece(s) of（…つの）、quart(s) of（…クオートの）、pint(s) of（…パイントの）、sheet(s) of（…枚の）、ton(s) of（…トンの）など

8

能力の度合いを示す　Levels of Ability Track 30

She **can** jump
very high.

He **can't** read it
without his glasses.

Can you really fly a
helicopter?

1. Melanie **can** play the flute very well.
   メラニーはフルートをとても上手に演奏できる。

2. We **cannot** finish on time.
   私たちは、時間どおりに終えられない。

3. **Could** you really eat that cake by yourself?
   あのケーキを本当に一人で食べられたのですか。

> 助動詞は動詞とともに用いられて、能力や可能性、必要性など、さまざまな意味をその動詞に付け加えることができる。その場合、助動詞とともに用いられる動詞は必ず原形となる。助動詞 can は「…することができる」という意味で、否定形は cannot（can't）、過去形は could、過去の否定形は could not（couldn't）となる。

可能性の度合いを示す　Levels of Probability Track 31

All the bags **will** fit in
the trunk.

I **might not** go on
the river rafting trip.

Would 3:00 this afternoon
be convenient for you?

1. The bus **might** get stuck in traffic.
   バスは交通渋滞につかまっているのかもしれない。

2. The cleaning person **will not** be in today.
   清掃員は、今日は来ないでしょう。

3. **Would** any of these desks be suitable for your office?
   ここにある机のどれかは、あなたのオフィスに向いていますか。

> 助動詞の may（might）は、「…かもしれない」という何かが起こる可能性を示し、will（would）は、「…だろう」と、ある程度の確信をもって未来のことを予想する場合に使われる。 must は「…に違いない」という強い可能性を示す。なお、might、would は必ずしも過去のことを意味するわけではない。

She **ought to** clean her desk.

People **shouldn't** ride on the grass.

Do we **have to** finish today?

1. You **ought to** try this soup.

   あなたは、このスープを飲んでみるべきです。

2. I **shouldn't** eat any more.

   私はもうこれ以上、食べない方がいい。

3. **Must** you make those strange noises?

   あなたは、その変な音を立てなければならないのですか。

> 「…しなければならない、…すべきだ」という義務を表す場合に使われる助動詞がいくつかある。 must は自分の意思でそう思っているときに、have (has) to はそれが規則だったり、仕方がないからしなければならなかったりするときに使われる。 ought to と should は、「義務ではないが…したほうがいい」という気持ちを表す。

Grammar Exercises

A　最初の文と逆の意味になるように、２番目の文の空欄に適切な語句を入れなさい。

[例] I will have a lot of free time. → I <u>won't</u> <u>have</u> a lot of free time.

1. I can translate the letter. → I _____ translate the letter.

2. Students shouldn't use a dictionary during the test. → Students _____ use a dictionary during the test.

3. We don't have to pay for the tickets to the game. → We _____ _____ pay for the tickets to the game.

4. Bikes must be left outside. → Bikes _____ _____ be left outside.

5. Guests have to return their trays after eating. → Guests _____ _____ _____ _____ return their trays after eating.

B （　　）内の正しい語を選び、文を完成させなさい。

1. The math problem is easy. I (can / can't) solve it.

2. We made the mess. We (must / ought / will) to clean it up.

3. The boy (shouldn't / couldn't) push the door open. It was too heavy.

4. (May / Would) I leave work early today? I need to go to the dentist.

5. To get a membership card, you (shall / can / have) to apply online.

C 次の文を読み、A と B のうちどちらの行動がとられる可能性が高いか選びなさい。

1. Some friends are going hiking tomorrow. Jack loves hiking. Tomorrow is his day off from work.
   (A) Jack can go hiking tomorrow.
   (B) Jack must not go with his friends tomorrow.

2. The restaurant is quiet at 6:30 PM. It gets very busy at 7:30 PM. It's hard to get a table then. Doris and her friends plan to eat there tonight.
   (A) To get a table, they must arrive at 7:30 PM.
   (B) To get a table, they should arrive at 6:30 PM.

3. Mike is going to a club on 5th Street. Parking is not allowed on that street. Parking is allowed on nearby streets.
   (A) Mike should park in front of the club.
   (B) Mike ought to park on 6th Street.

Skill Building

A **Listening**　3つの文(A, B, C)を聞き、それぞれの内容と一致しているイラストの下にその記号を書きなさい。　🎧 Track 33

1. _____　　　　2. _____　　　　3. _____

B **Speaking** 次の会話文を読み、以下のリストから適切な語 (句) を選んで空欄を埋めなさい。

| do | can't | should | I'll | has to |

Dora: I love Japanese food. But it looks kind of hard to make.

Tom: Actually, it isn't too difficult. That reminds me. I heard about a free cooking class. You ₁( ) sign up.

Dora: Hmm, maybe. ₂( ) you want to sign up, too?

Tom: It depends on the time. I work Monday and Wednesday nights. So I ₃( ) go on those nights.

Dora: For me, the class ₄( ) be on Thursday or Friday. Those are the only evenings I have free time.

Tom: Understood. ₅( ) look into it some more.

質問の答えとして最も適切なものを選びなさい。

1. ( ) What does Tom say about Japanese food?
   A: It's the most delicious type of food.
   B: It isn't hard to cook.
   C: Tom usually eats it for free.
   D: He and Dora should have it for lunch.

2. ( ) For a cooking class, which night would be best for both friends?
   A: Monday   B: Tuesday
   C: Wednesday   D: Thursday

C **Writing** ( ) 内の語句を並べ替え、正しい文を作りなさい。

1. You (Okinawa / a boat / could / to / take).

   _____

2. It (weekend / not / this / rain / might).

   _____

3. Should (to / bring / the party / we / food)?

   _____

A **Reading Passage**　次の英文を読み、（　）内の正しいほうの単語を選びなさい。

Many people live without the use of two arms. Some are born disabled. Others lose their arms through accidents or disease. But the human spirit is strong. ₁ <u>A lot of people (will / won't) never give up.</u> A perfect example is "foot and mouth painters."

True, they (cannot / couldn't) use their arms. But they (ought / can) still create beautiful paintings.

₂ <u>These special painters (must / have) work hard to learn their craft.</u> For example, take Huang Guofu of Chongqing, China. As a child, he lost the use of his arms. He later learned to paint with his foot, and then with his mouth. Now his work is shown in museums. Perhaps the most famous foot painter was Christy Brown (1932-1981). ₃ <u>The Irishman (could / shall) paint and write very well.</u> His story was told in the movie *My Left Foot*.

> **NOTES**　disabled「障害を負って」 disease「病気」 give up「(夢などを)あきらめる」
> craft「技術」 take「例として考える」 Chongqing「重慶」

B **Comprehension**　それぞれの文の内容が正しければ T(true) を、誤りであれば F(false) を○で囲みなさい。

1. People who don't have arms can still do great things.　　T　F

2. Huang Guofu was born without the use of his arms.　　T　F

3. Christy Brown had another talent besides painting.　　T　F

C **Translation** 前ページの英文の中で、下線が引かれている文を日本語に訳しなさい。

1. _____

2. _____

3. _____

Reference Material

助動詞の種類と機能 Chart of Modal Types and Functions

	意思・未来	能力	可能性	義務	許可	過去の習慣
can / could		…できる（できた）	…がありうる		…してよい	
may / might			…かもしれない		…してよい	
must / have to			…に違いない	…すべきだ		
shall	…するつもりだ			…すべきだ		
should / ought to			…のはずだ	…すべきだ		
will	…するつもりだ …だろう		…だろう			
would	…しようとした …だろう		…だろう			…したものだ
used to						…したものだ
need to				…する必要がある		

1. I **can** bring the beach towels and big umbrella.
2. We **may** leave during the intermission.
3. The street lights **must** be replaced every 12 years.
4. I **shall** tell you my decision as soon as I make it.
5. The kids **ought to** be more careful about where they play baseball.
6. My family **will** stay at the same campground as last time.
7. More people **would** study at the library if there were more tables.
8. There **used to** be a huge factory right where we're standing.
9. Do we **need to** change the car's oil before the road trip?

9 提案と命令 Suggestions and Commands

Let's を使った提案の表現　Suggestions Starting with "Let's"

Let's get some hot chocolate!

Let's order cherry pie for dessert.

Let's give our teacher a basket of apples.

1. **Let's** rent a movie.
   映画をレンタルしよう。

2. **Let's** invite Charlie to go with us.
   チャーリーを誘って一緒に行こう。

3. **Let's** not make a decision so quickly.
   そんなに早く決めないようにしよう。

> 「Let's ＋動詞」で、その場にいる人に対して「いっしょに…しよう（じゃないか）」と提案したり、勧誘したりすることができる。否定文で「…しないようにしよう」という場合は、「Let's not ＋ 動詞」という語順になる。

提案を表す動詞　Subject + "recommend / suggest / think"

The doctor **suggested** that I eat more vegetables.

I **think** we should cancel the picnic.

Mom **recommended** that I eat before the movie.

1. I **recommend** that you bring a jacket.
   上着を持ってくることをおすすめします。

2. Walt **didn't suggest** that we take the scenic route home. It was my idea.
   ウォルトが私たちに景色のよい道で帰ろうと提案したのではありません。それは私の考えでした。

3. **Do** you **think** I should buy the headphones?
   私はそのヘッドフォンを買うべきだと思いますか。

> recommend や suggest などの動詞は、提案や勧誘の意味で使うことができる。その場合、提案の内容を表す that 節内の動詞（例文では bring、take、buy）は原型のまま用いるか、should を付けることになる。なお、think を使う場合は常に should を付ける。

Track 36

Please sign your
name here.

Come take a look at
this document.

Don't tap on the glass,
or you'll bother the lion.

1. **Please** take off your shoes.
   靴を脱ぐようお願いします。

2. **Come** here for a moment.
   ちょっとこちらへ来てください。

3. **Don't** touch that, please.
   それに触れないでください。

> たいていの動詞はそのままの形で文頭に置くことにより、相手に対して「…しなさい」という命令や要求を表すことができる。ただし、please（どうぞ）を文頭か文末に追加することで、強い口調を和らげることができる。また「…してはいけない」という否定の命令文を作るには、「 Don't ＋ 動詞」という表現を使う。

Grammar Exercises

Ⓐ　（　）内に示された指示に従って、次の文を書き換えなさい。

[例]　You should park somewhere else.　（命令文に）　→　<u>Please park somewhere else.</u>

1. Take the train.　（提案を示す文に）

   I recommend that _____

2. I think we should look for a new roommate.　（let's を使った提案に）

   Let's _____

3. I think you should drive more carefully.　（命令文に）

   Please _____

4. I recommend that you speak more slowly.　（命令文に）

   _____, please.

5. Don't use your phone in class.　（忠告を示す文に）

   I don't think _____

B 次の文のあとに続く表現の記号を、空欄に書き入れなさい。

1. We're out of eggs. Let's _____   (A) hurry up and choose our books.

2. The library closes soon. Let's _____   (B) do the best job possible for him.

3. He is an important client. Let's _____   (C) buy an umbrella.

4. It's about to rain. Let's _____   (D) stop by the bank.

5. I need some cash. Let's _____   (E) go to the supermarket.

C 次の会話文の空欄に適当な語を入れなさい。

1. A: _____ throw a party next Friday.

   B: Good idea! Who should we invite?

2. A: Do you think I should get a new coffee maker?

   B: No, I _____ think you should. The one you have now is fine.

3. A: _____ turn down the television. I'm doing my homework.

   B: Sorry about that. I'll do it now.

Skill Building

A **Listening** 3つの文(A, B, C)を聞き、それぞれの内容と一致しているイラストの下にその記号を書きなさい。 🎧 Track 37

1. _____   2. _____   3. _____

B **Speaking**　次の会話文を読み、以下のリストから適切な語 (句) を選んで空欄を埋めなさい。

get	let's	go	suggested	do

Joe:　I can't decide what to do during winter break. My brother 1(　　　) that I earn some money.

Lisa:　That's one idea. But it was a really hard semester, and you deserve a break. 2(　　　) what makes you happy.

Joe:　I like the way you think! I never get the chance to ski anymore.

Lisa:　Then 3(　　　) skiing. My friend works at a travel agency. They just put out some fliers for winter vacation deals.

Joe:　Nice. Please 4(　　　) me some the next time you're there.

Lisa:　Actually, the agency is close by. 5(　　　) go over there now.

質問の答えとして最も適切なものを選びなさい。

1. (　) Who thinks Joe should get a job?
　　A: Lisa　　　　　　　　　B: Joe
　　C: Joe's brother　　　　　D: Lisa's friend

2. (　) What does Lisa suggest doing next?
　　A: Flying to a ski resort
　　B: Calling her friend about vacation deals
　　C: Finishing this semester's school work
　　D: Going to a travel agency

C **Writing**　次の会話で、話者 A に対する話者 B の返事を、( ) 内の語句を使って書きなさい。

1. A: I'm looking for a good hair stylist. Any ideas? (suggest, try, Studio Antonio)
　　B: I _____

2. A: What did Kurt recommend that you do? (recommended, speak with Nancy)
　　B: He _____

3. A: It's already 4:30. My package isn't here yet. (think, should, call the courier)
　　B: I _____

Grammar Through Reading

A **Reading Passage** 次の文章の空欄に、以下の語群からあてはまるものを選んで入れなさい。

| Go forward | Potatoes, please | Call Steve |

Robots are becoming a part of our daily lives. They build our cars, clean our floors, and even keep us company. The latest trend in robotics is voice control. We can already control many machines with our voices. Take some cell phones, for instance. Just say, "₁(_____) (_____)." Then the phone places the call.

Designers are also building voice functions into robots. Many are one-armed models. They can, for example, help disabled people. The user says, "₂(_____) (_____)." Then the robot picks up the food and feeds the person. Other robots are more complex. They can take many commands, like "₃(_____) (_____)," "Look up," "Turn right," etc. Such robots are very useful at home and work.

NOTES daily「毎日の」 keep company「遊び相手になる」 trend「流行」 robotics「ロボット工学」 place「(電話を)かける」 function「機能」 feed「食事をさせる」 command「命令」

B **Comprehension** それぞれの文の内容が正しければ T(true) を、誤りであれば F(false) を○で囲みなさい。

1. We cannot use voice commands to control machines yet.　　　　T　F

2. A robot feeds a person without any command from him or her.　　T　F

3. Some robots can understand many voice commands.　　　　T　F

C **Translation** 前ページの英文の中で、下線が引かれている文を日本語に訳しなさい。

1. _____

2. _____

3. _____

——— Reference Material ———

> 提案または命令を表すその他の表現 Other Useful Expressions

A) **I + 動詞 + that + you (should)... / I don't + 動詞 + that + you (should)...**

> この構文でよく使われる動詞のリスト：
> ask（求める）、suggest（勧める）、propose（提案する）、advise（アドバイスする）、insist（主張する）、command（命令する）、demand（要求する）、order（命令する）、recommend（推奨する）、request（要請する）、require（求める）、urge（強く要請する）、think（当然…だと思う）

   例： I think that you should accept his offer.

B) **Shall I...? / Shall we...?** （…しましょうか）
   例： Shall we get some coffee?

C) **Why don't you / we...** （…しませんか）
   例： Why don't you meet me there at 3:30.

D) **How about...?** （…してはどうですか）
   例： How about putting in energy efficient windows?

E) **If I were you, I would (I'd)...** （私があなたなら…するでしょう）
   例： If I were you, I'd listen to Owen.

F) **might** （…してはどうでしょう）
   例： You might consider getting a second opinion.

G) **should** （…するべきです）
   例： You should study harder.

H) **Be + 形容詞 / Don't be + 形容詞** （…でいなさい /…ではいけません）
   例： Be quiet! / Don't be shy.

I) **Never + 動詞の原形** （決して…してはいけません）
   例： Never forget the password!

J) **shall** （…しなさい）
   例： You shall do as you're told. / You shall not go any further.

K) **can** （…せよ）
   例： You can go now. / You can't stay here.

10 未来形 Simple Future Tense

近い未来を表す現在形・現在進行形 Expressed with Present Tenses Track 38

The store **closes** soon.

The ship **is leaving** shortly.

Are you **playing** golf again tomorrow?

1. The bus **arrives** in a few minutes.
   バスは数分後に到着することになっています。

2. **Are** you **doing** anything this weekend?
   今週末は何かする予定がありますか。

3. Hisano **is going to call** me at 5:00.
   ヒサノは5時に私に電話をかけてくるでしょう。

> 未来のことでも、起こることが確実な場合には現在形が使われる。また、動詞の現在進行形を使うと、「…することになっている」というように、今、準備していることが近い将来に起こることを表すことができる。さらに、「主語 + be going to + 動詞の原形」を使うと、「…するつもりである、…するだろう」というように、近い未来の予定や予測を表すことができる。

will ＋動詞の原形 Will + Original Verb Track 39

The race **will be** very close.

Someone **will fix** the air conditioner on Friday.

Will your parents **move** to this area?

1. The class **will end** early today.
   今日、授業は早く終わるでしょう。

2. All of us **will get** new shoes.
   私たちはみな、新しい靴を買うつもりです。

3. **Will** Chuck **be** at the office tomorrow?
   チャックは明日、会社に来るだろうか。

> それほど確実ではない未来について述べるときや、単に話者がそうなると思っているだけのときは、「主語＋ will ＋動詞の原形」で「…だろう」という表現を使うことになる。

Track 40

The elevator **won't stop** on the second floor.

We **aren't going to see** the movie today.

The seller **will not reduce** the price.

1. No, I **am not transferring** to another branch next month.

　いいえ、私は来月、別の支店に転勤する予定はありません。

2. It **isn't going to rain** this afternoon.

　今日の午後に雨は降らないでしょう。

3. They **won't go shopping** later.

　彼らは、このあと買い物に行かないでしょう。

> 未来形の否定文（…する予定はない、…しないだろう）は、be 動詞または will のうしろに not を付けて作る。いずれも isn't、aren't、won't のように短縮形が使われることが多い。

Grammar Exercises

Ⓐ　（　）内の指示に従って、次の文を書き換えなさい。

[例]　He will be home tomorrow.（否定文に）→ He will not be home tomorrow.

1. You will have a lot of free time.　（疑問文に）

_____

2. I play racquetball with Ricky.　（will を使った未来形に）

_____

3. John is giving a presentation next Thursday.　（否定文に）

_____

4. She is leading a tour group to Australia.　（疑問文に）

_____

5. The boat leaves soon.　（現在進行形を使った未来形に）

_____

B 未来のことについて述べている次の文の空欄に will、am、is または are を補いなさい。ただし、何も必要がないときは空欄のままにしておくこと。

[例]　We ＿＿＿＿＿ going to visit her next weekend.

　　　→ We <u>are</u> going to visit her next weekend.

1. He ＿＿＿＿＿ give us a ride to the airport.

2. No, I ＿＿＿＿＿ not doing anything later.

3. ＿＿＿＿＿ you be home this afternoon?

4. The plane ＿＿＿＿＿ departs in 45 minutes.

5. She ＿＿＿＿＿ moving to Miyazaki in August.

C　次の会話文の空欄に適当な語を入れなさい。

1. A: What ＿＿＿＿＿ ＿＿＿＿＿ doing over the holiday?

   B: I'm going ＿＿＿＿＿ spend some time with my niece.

2. A: I see your sale starts on the 18th. ＿＿＿＿＿ these pants be on sale, too?

   B: No, we just got those. They will ＿＿＿＿＿ be on sale.

3. A: ＿＿＿＿＿ Mary going with you to Berlin?

   B: It's mostly a business trip. So I ＿＿＿＿＿ probably go alone.

─────────────── **Skill Building** ───────────────

A **Listening**　3つの文 (A, B, C) を聞き、それぞれの内容と一致しているイラストの下にその記号を書きなさい。　🎧 Track 41

1. ＿＿＿＿＿　　　　　2. ＿＿＿＿＿　　　　　3. ＿＿＿＿＿

64

| won't | will | am | is | will |

Stephen: I'm surprised to see you at the mall, Kate. Don't you work tonight?

Kate: I do. In fact, I $_1$( ) leaving in a minute.

Stephen: OK. $_2$( ) you be at Mark's party this weekend?

Kate: I $_3$( ), unfortunately. I have to work Saturday night.

Stephen: That's too bad. Oh, you know what. Mark $_4$( ) going to film the party. He $_5$( ) probably upload it to YouTube.

Kate: Cool! I look forward to seeing it.

質問の答えとして最も適切なものを選びなさい。

1. ( ) Who is going to work tonight?
    A: Stephen   B: Mark
    C: Kate   D: Stephen's boss

2. ( ) Why won't Kate go to the party?
    A: She has to work that night.
    B: She needs to help Stephen on Saturday.
    C: She will film something all day and night.
    D: She is going to the movies.

C Writing ( ) 内の単語を並べ替え、正しい文を作りなさい。

1. The (in / ends / minutes / opera / five).

_____

2. We (leaving / 3:00 / not / until / are).

_____

3. Will (be / Monday / museum / open / the / on)?

_____

A **Reading Passage** 次の英文を読み、(　)内の正しいほうの語(句)を選びなさい。

₁In 100 years, cities (will be / are) very different. We can expect them to be quieter, cleaner, and safer. More people will drive electric cars. That will reduce noise and air pollution. ₂Also, city streets (are going / will) to have many more cameras. They will be on most large streets. That should help reduce crime.

However, the future is (no / not) going to be all positive. For example, many people do not like street cameras. They feel having cameras everywhere reduces our privacy.

₃Also, in the future more people (leave / will leave) rural areas. They will (move / moving) to cities. That may make cities very crowded. Funding places like schools and hospitals will also be a challenge. That will be true for both cities and rural areas.

NOTES expect A to be B「AがBとなると予想する」 reduce「減らす」 air pollution「大気汚染」 positive「好ましい、明るい」 rural「地方の、田舎の」

B **Comprehension** それぞれの文の内容が正しければ T(true) を、誤りであれば F(false) を○で囲みなさい。

1. The passage says cities will be safer in the future. T　F

2. Street cameras are already everywhere. T　F

3. In the future, rural areas will have fewer people. T　F

1. _____

2. _____

3. _____

Reference Material

(be 動詞 + about to)

1. I **am about to** drive to Daniel's house.

2. They **aren't about to** change the policy.

3. **Is** the gallery **about to** close?

4. We **are not about to** redecorate the hotel because of one bad review.

> 「be about to ＋ 動詞の原形」で、「まさに…しようとしている」という意味に
> なり、be going to よりも差し迫った未来を表す。また、be going to とは違って、
> tomorrow や next month、at 5:00 など、未来の時を表す副詞（句）とともに
> は使われないのがふつうである。否定文は、「be ＋ not about to ＋動詞の原形」
> という形をとり、「…しそうにない」のように、ある状況が起こったり、ある行
> 為が行われたりする可能性の低いことを表す。

(未来形の否定疑問文　Negative Questions)

1. **Aren't** you **coming** with us to Nagano?

2. **Won't** you **join** us on our walk?

3. **Won't** the city **put on** a big fireworks show this year?

4. **Isn't** the zoo **getting** some pandas soon?

> 未来形の否定疑問文を使って、「…しないのですか」と確認を求めたり、「…し
> ませんか」と勧誘をしたりすることができる。

Track 42

Where is the court house?

Who ate half the chocolate cake?

When will the bus get here?

1. **What** is your name?
   あなたのお名前は何ですか。

2. **Why** didn't Bill turn off the lights?
   なぜビルは灯りを消していなかったのですか。

3. **Where** will they go during Golden Week?
   彼らはゴールデンウィーク中、どこに行く予定なのですか。

> 疑問詞を使った疑問文では、疑問詞が文の先頭に置かれる。疑問詞が主語となっている場合では動詞が続き、それ以外の場合は主語と助動詞が倒置された文が続く。

How を使った疑問文　Compound Phrases with "How"
 Track 43

How many calories are in one serving?

How often does the museum change exhibits?

How much does this washing machine cost?

1. **How long** is the flight?
   飛行時間はどれくらいの長さですか。

2. **How many** people can fit in the car?
   その車には何人が乗れますか。

3. **How often** do you get a health checkup?
   あなたは、どれくらいの間隔で健康診断を受けますか。

> how のうしろに状態を表す形容詞や副詞を続けて、さまざまな疑問文を作ることができる。長さを尋ねるときの How long、数を尋ねるときの How many、頻度を尋ねるときの How often、値段を尋ねるときの How much などは、その例である。

There is enough room in the back, **isn't there**?

This plant needs a lot of sunshine, **doesn't it**?

You aren't thinking about moving, **are you**?

1. **Cathy isn't quitting** her job, **is she**?
   キャシーが仕事を辞めることはないですよね。

2. **There wasn't** any food in the refrigerator, **was there**?
   冷蔵庫の中には何も食べ物が入ってなかったですよね。

3. **There are** some famous actors in the movie, **aren't there**?
   その映画には、有名な役者が何人か出演していますよね。

付加疑問文とは、「…ですよね」「…ではないですよね」のように、相手に軽く念を押したり、同意を求めたりするために文末に追加される疑問文のこと。否定文には肯定の疑問を付け、肯定文には否定の疑問を付ける。主文に be 動詞が使われていればその be 動詞を、一般動詞や助動詞が使われていれば、時制や人称に応じて do / does / did や will や can などを使う。また、付加疑問文の中では、主語に対応した代名詞が用いられるが there 構文では there をそのまま使う。

Grammar Exercises

Ⓐ　（　　）内の正しい語を選び、文を完成させなさい。

1. (Where / Who / What) do you go to school?

2. How (long / much / many) time do we have?

3. (When / What / Whom) are they going to the farmer's market?

4. (Who / Where / What) is that man over there?

5. How (much / often / many) do you visit your aunt?

6. (Why / What / Who) is the road closed?

7. How (many / long / often) people are waiting in line?

8. (What / When / Where) are you doing this afternoon?

B 次の文に、付加疑問文を加えなさい。

[例] It's a good class, (　　　　　) (　　　　　)? → It's a good class, <u>isn't</u> <u>it</u>?

1. Slovenia is a beautiful country, (　　　　　) (　　　　　)?

2. The 100 yen shop closes at 8:00, (　　　　　) (　　　　　)?

3. You were born in Tokyo, (　　　　　) (　　　　　)?

4. They won't be late, (　　　　　) (　　　　　)?

5. The school doesn't have a website, (　　　　　) (　　　　　)?

6. Ben will meet us for breakfast, (　　　　　) (　　　　　)?

C 次の会話文の空欄に適当な語を入れなさい。

1. A: _____ did you open the window?
   B: Because it's hot in here.

2. A: How _____ bags do you have?
   B: I have two suitcases to check in. Also, I can take a bag on the
      plane, _____ I?

3. A: How _____ foreign languages does Frances speak?
   B: Let's see.... I know she speaks Spanish. She also speaks Italian,
      _____ she?

────────────────── **Skill Building** ──────────────────

A **Listening**　3つの文(A, B, C)を聞き、それぞれの内容と一致しているイラストの
下にその記号を書きなさい。　🎧 Track 45

1. _____　　　　　2. _____　　　　　3. _____

B **Speaking** 次の会話文を読み、以下のリストから適切な語 (句) を選んで空欄を埋めなさい。

| where | isn't it | what | why | how much |

Akihito: ₁(　　　　　) do you think? Should I enter the violin competition?

Judy: ₂(　　　　　) not? You're an excellent violinist. Besides, it's open to everybody, ₃(　　　　　)? I say go for it!

Akihito: Thanks. To be honest, I don't expect to win. But it could be fun.

Judy: Exactly. ₄(　　　　　) time do you have to prepare?

Akihito: About a month. But I can't practice at home. ₅(　　　　　) do you suggest I go?

Judy: You can practice at my place. I have plenty of room.

質問の答えとして最も適切なものを選びなさい。

1. (　) What does Akihito think about the competition?
　　A: He will probably win. 　B: He needs more time to prepare.
　　C: He shouldn't enter. 　D: He might have a good time.

2. (　) What does Judy offer Akihito?
　　A: Free violin lessons 　B: A ride to the competition
　　C: A place to practice 　D: Help with the entrance fee

C **Writing** 次の文につき、(　　) 内の語句を使って疑問文を作りなさい。

[例] They are going on vacation. (where, vacation)
　　→ <u>Where are they going on vacation?</u>

1. We don't have very much rice. (how much, have)

_____

2. The festival ends soon. (when, end)

_____

3. On weekends, many people go to Harajuku. (Harajuku is crowded, it)

_____

A **Reading Passage** 次の英文を読み、(　) 内の正しいほうの単語を選びなさい。

Not long ago, access to information was limited. There were millions of books available. But people had to go to libraries to do research. ₁That takes a lot of time, (isn't / doesn't) it? On top of that, local libraries don't always have the books people need.

Another problem is remembering information. Some people have bad memories. (How / Why) can they remember a lot of details? Finally, there is a practical question. Even if you want to learn a lot, how (many / much) books can one person read?

With the Internet, we live in a new world of limitless information. You can find out almost anything, anytime. ₂That's amazing, (can't / isn't) it? But there is a problem. People aren't reading as many books as they used to. To find answers to questions, they rely on websites like Google. That makes some people wonder: Is the Internet making us smarter or dumber? ₃(What / How) is your opinion?

NOTES do research「調べものをする」 memory「記憶」 detail「詳細、細部」 practical「現実的な」 limitless「限界がない」 rely on ...「…に頼る」 dumb「愚かな」

B **Comprehension** それぞれの文の内容が正しければ T(true) を、誤りであれば F(false) を○で囲みなさい。

1. Before we had the Internet, doing research was faster. T F

2. The Internet is leading to less book reading. T F

3. Everyone feels the Internet is making us smarter. T F

C **Translation**　前ページの英文の中で、下線が引かれている文を日本語に訳しなさい。

1. ＿＿＿＿＿＿＿＿＿＿＿＿＿＿＿＿＿＿＿＿＿＿＿＿＿＿＿＿＿＿

2. ＿＿＿＿＿＿＿＿＿＿＿＿＿＿＿＿＿＿＿＿＿＿＿＿＿＿＿＿＿＿

3. ＿＿＿＿＿＿＿＿＿＿＿＿＿＿＿＿＿＿＿＿＿＿＿＿＿＿＿＿＿＿

Reference Material

疑問詞の種類　List of Question Words

how（どのように）、what（何を）、when（いつ）、where（どこへ・どこで）、which（どちらを）、who（だれが）、whom（だれに・だれを）、whose（だれの）、why（なぜ）

疑問詞に他の単語を付けた疑問文　Other Compound Phrases Used at the Start of Sentences

How, What, Which, Whose などの疑問詞は、別の単語と組み合わせることで、さまざまな疑問文を作ることができる。

・How ＋ 形容詞（＋名詞）...? ／ How ＋ 副詞 （どれくらいの）
この形で、あるものの数量や状態などを尋ねることができる。
How many、How much、How often、How long、How old、How big、How tall、How fast、How far、How soon などがよく使われる。
〔例〕How much money do you have?

・What ＋ 名詞 ...? （どの）
この形では、「どれが、なにが」と尋ねる疑問文を作ることができる。
What kind of、What time、What day などがその例。
〔例〕What kind of music do you like?

・Which ＋ 名詞 ...? （どちらの）
いくつか比べるものがあって、「どちらの」と尋ねる場合、Which のあとにその名詞を続ける。
〔例〕Which movie would you like to see?

・Whose ＋ 名詞 ...? （だれの）
〔例〕Whose phone is this?

12 形容詞 Adjectives

名詞を修飾する形容詞　Preceding Nouns Track 46

It's an **old** piece of jewelry.

That isn't a **fast** train.

Should I just bring my **small** suitcase?

1. What a **pretty** dog!
   なんてかわいい犬なんでしょう！

2. It isn't my **favorite** brand.
   それは私の好みのブランドではありません。

3. Do you carry **blue** jackets?
   青いジャケットは、この店にありますか。

> 形容詞には、名詞の前に置かれてその名詞を説明したり、持続的な性質や状態を表したりする働きがある。これを「形容詞の限定用法」と言う。

主語の状態を表す形容詞　Following Linking Verbs Track 47

The speaker looks **confident**.

The TV doesn't appear **broken**.

Did you get **tired** from climbing the stairs?

1. That hiker looks **lost**.
   あのハイカーは道に迷っているようだ。

2. I don't feel **nervous**.
   私は緊張していません。

3. Does this yogurt taste **strange** to you?
   このヨーグルトは、あなたには変な味ですか。

> 形容詞が、be 動詞や主語の状態・感覚を表す動詞のあとに用いられた場合は、その主語の一時的な状態を表すことになる。これは「形容詞の叙述用法」と言う。

Track 48

The man is following **several** horses.

There aren't **a lot of** people there.

Can I have **some** water, please?

1. Sure, I have **a little** time.
   いいですよ。少しなら時間があります。

2. The new student doesn't have **many** friends.
   その新入生は、あまり友達がいない。

3. Does the pet shop have **any** songbirds?
   そのペットショップには、鳴き鳥がいますか。

> 数量形容詞には、複数形の普通名詞の前に置かれて数の大小を表すものと、物質名詞または抽象名詞の前に置かれて量や程度の大小を表すものがある。

Grammar Exercises

Ⓐ　（　）内の正しい語を選び、文を完成させなさい。

1. This pudding (tastes / feels) great. Did you make it yourself?

2. I love this photo. You (sound / look) happy standing there on the Brooklyn Bridge.

3. It (smells / turns) strange in here. There might be a gas leak.

4. Just tell me the truth. I won't (sound / get) angry.

5. He (appears / keeps) confused. Show him how to use the device.

6. I love your plan. It (sounds / becomes) perfect to me!

7. Do you (get / feel) all right? Your face is completely white.

8. It doesn't (seem / be) fair. She's going shopping. The rest of us have to clean the house.

B　次の文のあとに続く表現の記号を、空欄に書き入れなさい。

1. That book is wonderful. It's _____
2. He loves sports. So I bought him _____
3. She's going swimming. That's why she has _____
4. My fingers are not very big. I'll take _____
5. We want to go to Bali. Can you recommend _____

(A) a new baseball glove.

(B) this small silver ring.

(C) a good travel agent?

(D) my favorite story.

(E) that big towel.

C　次の文を読み、その内容を正しく表しているものを A と B のどちらかから選びなさい。

1. George works from Monday to Saturday. He also works on holidays.
   (A) George has a lot of free time.
   (B) George has little free time.

2. There were 500 tickets for the event. Nearly 490 are already sold.
   (A) There are many tickets left.
   (B) There are few tickets left.

3. John made eight bottles of hot sauce. He gave them all to friends.
   (A) John doesn't have any more hot sauce.
   (B) John still has some hot sauce.

Skill Building

A **Listening**　3つの文(A, B, C)を聞き、それぞれの内容と一致しているイラストの下にその記号を書きなさい。　🎧 Track 49

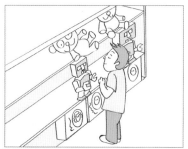
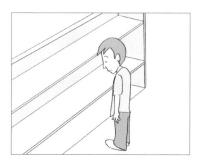

1. _____　　　2. _____　　　3. _____

whole	a few	tired	smells	lots of

Al:　　I'm glad you could join me for dinner. But you look

　　　　$_1($　　　　　　). Is everything all right?

Flora:　I'm fine, thanks. Two of my co-workers are on vacation. So I

　　　　have $_2($　　　　　) cases to handle.

Al:　　When will they be back?

Flora:　In $_3($　　　　　　) days, fortunately. Then I plan to sleep the

　　　　$_4($　　　　　) weekend!

Al:　　I don't blame you. A long rest always makes me feel better.

Flora:　Me, too. Well, we don't have to talk about work tonight. The

　　　　food $_5($　　　　　) delicious. Let's eat!

質問の答えとして最も適切なものを選びなさい。

1. (　　) What will Flora do after her co-workers return?
　　　A: Sleep a long time　　　　　B: Cook a big dinner
　　　C: Handle their cases　　　　　D: Work on Saturday

2. (　　) What does Flora want to do next?
　　　A: Talk about Al's job　　　　　B: Go on vacation
　　　C: Eat dinner　　　　　　　　　D: Return to the office

C Writing　（　　）内の単語を並べ替え、正しい文を作りなさい。

1. You (a / have / home / beautiful).

　　＿＿＿＿＿＿＿＿＿＿＿＿＿＿＿＿＿＿＿＿＿＿＿＿＿＿

2. The (smell / doesn't / fresh / fruit).

　　＿＿＿＿＿＿＿＿＿＿＿＿＿＿＿＿＿＿＿＿＿＿＿＿＿＿

3. Are (many / club / there / in the / people)?

　　＿＿＿＿＿＿＿＿＿＿＿＿＿＿＿＿＿＿＿＿＿＿＿＿＿＿

A **Reading Passage**　次の英文を読み、（　）内の正しいほうの語(句)を選びなさい。

Did you know that (much / many) inventions were accidents? Penicillin and post-it notes are two famous examples. Another is the chocolate chip cookie. It was invented by an American woman, Ruth Wakefield.

With her husband, Mrs. Wakefield ran the Toll House Inn. She also made meals for the guests. One evening in 1930, she was preparing chocolate cookies. But she didn't have enough baking chocolate. So she broke apart (some / much) Nestle chocolate and mixed it in. ₁It was (a lucky / an unlucky) decision. ₂The cookies (got / tasted) great!

The cookies soon became popular. Later, Mrs. Wakefield made a deal with Nestle. They put her recipe on every package of chocolate chips. ₃In return, she got (free / freedom) chocolate for life.

> **NOTES**　invention「発明、発明品」 accident「偶然の産物」 post-it note「付箋紙」
> run「経営する」 baking chocolate「料理用チョコレート」 make a deal「契約する」
> recipe「レシピ、作り方」 for life「一生の間」

B **Comprehension**　それぞれの文の内容が正しければ T(true) を、誤りであれば F(false) を○で囲みなさい。

1. The passage does not mention clothing inventions.　　　　T　F

2. Guests at the Toll House Inn probably ate Mrs. Wakefield's cookies.　　　　T　F

3. Nestle gave Mrs. Wakefield a lot of money.　　　　T　F

ⓒ Translation 前ページの英文の中で、下線が引かれている文を日本語に訳しなさい。

1. _____

2. _____

3. _____

───── **Reference Material** ─────

主語と主語を修飾する形容詞をつなぐ動詞　List of Linking Verbs Preceding Adjectives

appear（…のように見える）、be（…である）、become（…になる）、feel（…と感じる）、get（…の状態になる）、keep（…のままでいる）、look（…のように見える）、remain（…のままでいる）、seem（…のように思われる）、smell（…のにおいがする）、sound（…のように思われる）、taste（…の味がする）、turn（…になる）など

数量形容詞の種類　List of Quantifiers

1) 加算名詞に付くもの：　　both（両方の）、either（どちらか一方の）、neither（どちらも…でない）、each（それぞれの）、every（あらゆる）、a few（多少の）、few（わずかの）、several（いくつかの）、many（多くの）
2) 不可算名詞に付くもの：　a little（少量の）、little（ほとんどない）、much（たくさんの）
3) どちらの名詞にも付くもの：all（すべての）、some（いくらかの）、any（いくらかの）、no（まったくない）、enough（十分な）、more（もっと）、most（ほとんどの）、plenty of（たくさんの）、a lot of (lots of)（たくさんの）

名詞のあとに置かれる形容詞　Adjectives Following Nouns

1) something（何か）、anything（何か）、everything（すべてのもの）、nothing（何も…ない）を修飾する形容詞
2) somewhere（どこか）、anywhere（どこか）、everywhere（どこでも）、nowhere（どこでも…ない）を修飾する形容詞
3) someone（だれか）、somebody（だれか）、anyone（だれか）、anybody（だれか）、everyone（みんな）、everybody（みんな）、no one（だれも…ない）、nobody（だれも…ない）を修飾する形容詞
4) -ible、-able で終わる形容詞や、asleep や present などのように慣用的に名詞の後に置かれる形容詞

形容詞となる現在分詞と過去分詞　Present vs. Past Participles

1. The book looks **interesting**. ／ She is **interested** in the book.
2. The idea wasn't **exciting**. ／ We weren't **excited** by the idea.
3. Was it a **surprising** decision? ／ Were you **surprised** by the decision?

いくつかの動詞の現在分詞と過去分詞は、形容詞として使うことができる。ただし、それぞれで意味が異なるので注意が必要である。

13 比較 **Comparatives**

〜と同じくらい as ... as ...

Track 50

Jenny is **as** tall **as** Tina.

I don't play chess **as** well **as** my father.

Are their cakes **as** delicious **as** their cookies?

1. My phone is **as** small **as** yours.
   私の電話は、あなたのと同じくらい小さい。

2. Silver is not **as** valuable **as** gold.
   銀は、金ほど価値が高くない。

3. Is this piano **as** good **as** the other one?
   このピアノは、もうひとつのと同じくらい上等ですか。

> 2つのものを比較する場合、「A + be 動詞 + as 形容詞 as + B」という構文で、「A は B と同じくらい〜だ」という意味を表すことができる。否定形では、「not so 形容詞 as」の形も使われる。

比較 Comparatives

Track 51

The dog is **bigger than** the cat.

It isn't **more expensive than** the other restaurant.

Was the flight **less crowded than** you expected?

1. Horses are **stronger than** sheep.
   ウマはヒツジよりも力が強い。

2. Today's test wasn't **harder than** last week's.
   今日の試験は先週のものより易しかった。

3. Is Doug **more experienced than** Tina?
   ダグはティナよりも経験が豊富ですか。

> 2つのものを比較する場合、「A + be 動詞 + 形容詞の比較級 + than B」という構文で、「A は B よりも〜だ」という意味を表すことができる。一般に形容詞の比較級は、-er を語尾に付けて作るものと、形容詞の前に more または less を付けて作るものの2種類がある。ただし、easy や busy のように y で終わる2音節の形容詞は、最後の y を i に変えたうえで -er を付ける。

Track 52

Martin is the **strongest** person on our team.

It isn't the **largest** house around, but we love it.

Can I please have the **least spicy** curry?

1. It was the **funniest** movie of the year!
   それは、今年で一番おもしろい映画だった。

2. She isn't the **slowest** runner in the group.
   彼女はそのグループで一番足の遅いランナーではありません。

3. Isn't this the museum's **most famous** sculpture?
   これは、この美術館にある最も有名な彫刻ではありませんか。

> 複数のものの中で「A が最も〜だ」ということを、「A ＋ be 動詞 ＋ the 形容詞の最上級 ＋ 名詞」という構文で表すことができる。形容詞の最上級は、一般に -est を語尾に付けて作るものと、形容詞の前に the most または the least を付けて作るものの 2 種類がある。ただし、funny のように y で終わる 2 音節の形容詞は、最後の y を i に変えたうえで -est を付ける。

Grammar Exercises

Ⓐ （　）内の形容詞を必要に応じて適当な形に変えて空欄に入れ、文を完成させなさい。

[例] This apartment is _____ than mine. (large)

　　→ This apartment is <u>larger</u> than mine.

1. For Atsushi, math is _____ than science. (hard)

2. Our city has three movie theaters. This one is huge. It's the _____ one. (big)

3. Your old car was as _____ as a boat! (wide)

4. Good health is more _____ than money. (important)

5. My office is _____ than this one. It's so bright in here. (dark)

6. Max is the _____ person in class. Nobody is as funny. (funny)

7. I'm not as _____ as my brother. (fast)

8. Lily is the most _____ person I know. (cheerful)

81

B 次のリストは、「形容詞、比較級、最上級」の順に並べたものである。空欄を埋めて、このリストを完成させなさい。

[例] big, bigger, _____ → big, bigger, <u>biggest</u>

1. easy, _____, easiest

2. smart, smarter, _____

3. popular, more popular, _____

4. _____, cuter, cutest

5. common, _____, most common

C 次の文を読み、その内容を正しく表しているものをAとBのどちらかから選びなさい。

1. Ted's house has three rooms. Jeff's house has six rooms.
   (A) Jeff's house is smaller than Ted's.
   (B) Ted's house is smaller than Jeff's.

2. Pencils cost 100 yen. Pens cost 125 yen. Markers cost 140 yen.
   (A) Pencils are cheaper than pens.
   (B) Pens are as expensive as markers.

3. The Nile River is 6,695 km long. The Amazon River is 6,400 km long. The Volga River is 3,700 km long.
   (A) The Amazon River is longer than the Nile River.
   (B) The Volga River is the shortest of the three.

───────────────── **Skill Building** ─────────────────

A **Listening**　3つの文(A, B, C)を聞き、それぞれの内容と一致しているイラストの下にその記号を書きなさい。　🎧 Track 53

1. _____　　　　2. _____　　　　3. _____

B Speaking 次の会話文を読み、以下のリストから適切な単語を選んで空欄を埋めなさい。

as	cheapest	longer	cheaper	as

Customer: What's the difference between these two computers?

Salesperson: Well, the X20 is ₁( ) fast ₂( ) the Z30. But the Z30 is heavier.

Customer: They're a bit expensive. Are there any ₃( ) models?

Salesperson: I'm afraid not. These are the ₄( ) ones we have.

Customer: OK. Just one last thing. How long do the batteries last?

Salesperson: The Z30 has a better battery. It lasts ₅( ) than the X20's battery. That's also why the Z30 is heavier.

質問の答えとして最も適切なものを選びなさい。

1. (   ) What point about each computer is not discussed?
   A: The color   B: The price
   C: The speed   D: The battery

2. (   ) Which of these is true?
   A: The shop has some computers that cost less than these models.
   B: The X20 and Z30 weigh about the same.
   C: For someone needing a good battery, the X20 would be best.
   D: Both computers run at the same speed.

C Writing 以下に示す2つの文を、(   )内の単語を使って1つの文にしなさい。

1. Your house is clean. / Mine isn't so clean. (than)

   Your house _____

2. Tom is tall. / Arthur is the same height. (as)

   Tom is _____

3. Geneva is expensive. / No other city in Europe is so expensive. (most)

   Geneva is the _____

Grammar Through Reading

Ⓐ Reading Passage　次の英文を読み、（　）内の正しいほうの単語を選びなさい。

New York and London are both famous cities. They have a lot in common. Both cities are rich in culture. They have many museums, theaters, and parks. ₁In that way, London is as interesting (as / than) New York. Also, they both welcome millions of tourists every year. So, London may be as popular as New York.

But the two cities also have big differences. London is 2,000 years old. New York is about one-fifth that age. ₂So, the British capital is much (old / older / oldest) than the Big Apple. On the other hand, there are 19 million people in New York. London has around 12 million residents. ₃That makes New York (more / most) crowded than London.

NOTES　both「どちらも」 in common「共通して」 museum「博物［美術］館」 theater「劇場」 tourist「観光客」 may（＋動詞の原形）「…かもしれない」 one-fifth「5分の1」 on the other hand「その一方で」 resident「住民」

Ⓑ Comprehension　それぞれの文の内容が正しければ T(true) を、誤りであれば F(false) を○で囲みなさい。

1. About 12 million people visit London every year.　　　　　T　F

2. The article says New York has more museums than London.　T　F

3. Twenty million people live in England's capital.　　　　　T　F

84

C **Translation**　前ページの英文の中で、下線が引かれている文を日本語に訳しなさい。

1. _____

2. _____

3. _____

— Reference Material —

比較級・最上級の作り方　More Notes about Comparatives

(1) 音節が 1 つだけの形容詞・副詞にはたいてい -er /-est を語尾に付ける。ただし、語尾が「短母音 ＋ 子音」の場合、最後の子音を重ねて、-er / -est を付ける。
taller, faster, bigger, fatter

(2) 2 音節以上の語の形容詞・副詞の多くは「more / most ＋ 形容詞」という形を用いる。

(3) 2 音節の形容詞・副詞でも、次のものは通例 -er / -est をとる。

(a) -er [-ure], -y, -le, -ow, -ly (形容詞) で終わるもの：
clever, obscure, happy, gentle, narrow, friendly

(b) 第 2 音節にアクセントがあるもの：
divine, remote

(c) –er / -est も可能だが、more / most を用いる傾向の強いもの：
common, cruel, handsome, pleasant, polite, solid, wicked

(4) 音節が 1 つの場合でも more / most を用いる場合があるもの：real, strange, like, right, wrong

(5) 叙述用法の形容詞にはたいてい more / most を用いる：fond, afraid, fearful, alone

(6) 固有名詞に由来する形容詞、形容詞として用いられる現在分詞・過去分詞、-ly の語尾をもつ副詞にはふつう more / most を用いる。

(7) 通例は -er によって比較級をつくる形容詞でも、比較級が 2 つ以上並置されると more を用いることが多い。
There never was a more kind and just man. 「これ以上親切で正しい人はいなかった」

(8) 程度の上下がつけられない形容詞やそれ自体に比較の要素を含む形容詞には、比較級や最上級は使われない。
perfect, absolute, unique, final, main, preferable など

(9) 副詞・叙述用法の形容詞には the をつけないことが多い：
You are most welcome.

(10) 複数の形容詞を併置するときは音節数に関係なく、most 1 つで統一することが多い。
She was the most innocent, gentle, and delightful person that I ever knew.

動詞を修飾する Modifying Verbs Track 54

The race leader is driving **quickly**.

He isn't singing **quietly**.

Is it still raining **heavily**?

1. Hideo speaks **slowly**.
   ヒデオは（いつも）ゆっくりしゃべる。

2. The traveler was in a rush and didn't pack the suitcase **carefully**.
   その旅行者はとても急いでいたので、スーツケースを注意深く詰めなかった。

3. Are you leaving **already**?
   あなたは、もう帰るのですか。

> 副詞は動詞とともに用いられて、その動詞の意味を修飾する働きがある。副詞を置く位置は比較的自由だが、動詞に目的語がある場合は、その目的語のうしろに置かれる。

形容詞を修飾する Modifying Adjectives Track 55

She is **almost** ready to leave.

The theater isn't **very** big.

Is it an **especially** rare piece?

1. John is **very** tall.
   ジョンは、とても背が高い。

2. The story wasn't **entirely** true.
   その話は、すべてが真実というわけではない。

3. Is this box big **enough**?
   この箱は十分な大きさですか。

> 副詞は形容詞の意味を強めたり程度を表したりするために、その形容詞の直前に置かれる。ただし、enough は例外で、形容詞のあとに置かれる。

**We frequently eat
at this restaurant.**

**He doesn't usually
take the train.**

**Did they collect the
garbage yesterday?**

1. We **often** take walks near the tea fields.

   私たちはよく茶畑の近くを散歩します。

2. I won't have lunch with Samuel **tomorrow**.

   私は明日、サミュエルとは昼食を食べる予定はない。

3. Can you please put the boxes over **there**?

   その箱は、あちらに置いていただけますか。

> often（しばしば）や always（いつも）などの頻度を表す副詞は主語のすぐあとに置かれることが多く、tomorrow（明日）や yesterday（昨日）などの時を表す副詞と here（ここ）や there（あそこ）などの場所を表す副詞は文末に置かれることが多い。なお、時を表す副詞と場所を表す副詞が 1 つの同じ文の中で使われているときは、場所が先に来ることが多い。

Grammar Exercises

A　（　）内の正しい語を選び、文を完成させなさい。

1. I see the elevator. It's over (there / that).

2. He (always / never) takes milk with his coffee. He prefers it black.

3. The door isn't (almost / very) wide. The sofa might not fit through.

4. Her songs are all (good / well) written.

5. Let's go (somewhere / nowhere) else. This place is too crowded.

6. Is that piece of wood (enough long / long enough)?

7. They aren't ready to start (already / yet).

8. Mr. Takara checked the document (carefully / careful).

B （　）内の単語を副詞に変えて空欄に入れなさい。

[例] It's a _____ growing trend. (quick) → It's a <u>quickly</u> growing trend.

1. The child _____ opened the present. (excited)

2. Their selection of reggae music is _____ good. (fair)

3. Passengers on a train should speak _____. (quiet)

4. The joke was _____ funny. (extreme)

5. Do you shop here _____? (regular)

C　次の文を読み、その内容を正しく表しているものを A と B のどちらかから選びなさい。

1. From Monday to Friday, Leon has French class every evening. Plus, he sometimes has private classes on the weekend.
   (A) Leon frequently studies French.
   (B) Leon rarely studies French.

2. I went to every store in town. None of them had that kind of paper.
   (A) The paper is sold everywhere.
   (B) The paper isn't sold anywhere.

3. I packed all my winter clothes into one box. I had to sit on it to close it!
   (A) The box was partially filled.
   (B) The box was completely filled.

Skill Building

A Listening　3つの文(A, B, C)を聞き、それぞれの内容と一致しているイラストの下にその記号を書きなさい。　🎧 Track 57

1. _____　　　　2. _____　　　　3. _____

| tomorrow | enough | always | beautifully | so |

Lita: I heard last night's concert was a big hit.

Pete: It was ₁(   ) amazing, Lita. Can you believe it? The room wasn't big ₂(   ). People were standing along the wall.

Lita: Wow! I wanted to go. But I ₃(   ) work on Thursdays.

Pete: That's OK – I know. We want to set up some weekend shows soon.

Lita: That would be great. Are you practicing ₄(   )? I'm free all day.

Pete: We are. You can hear our new pianist. He plays ₅(   ).

質問の答えとして最も適切なものを選びなさい。

1. (   ) During the concert, why did people stand along the wall?
    A: The room didn't have much space.
    B: The stage was close to the wall.
    C: The concert was very loud.
    D: The rest of the room was for dancing.

2. (   ) What is Lita planning to do tomorrow?
    A: Watch the band practice   B: Play the piano
    C: Work all day   D: Set up a show

C Writing (   ) 内の語句を並べ替え、正しい文を作りなさい。

1. It (snowing / heavily / is).

_____

2. The (completely / isn't / dry / paint).

_____

3. Did (driving test / yesterday / you / the / pass)?

_____

A **Reading Passage** 次の英文を読み、（　）内の正しいほうの単語を選びなさい。

Quilt making is a (very / much) famous American handicraft. It has a practical origin. A quilt is a type of three-piece bedding. The inner and outer layers are made of cloth. ₁The inside section contains a warm filling such as feathers.

Hundreds of years ago, few Americans were well-off. ₂They (seldom / carefully) reused everything, including scraps of cloth. Squares of cloth were sewn together. They became the quilt's inner and outer layers. This was a so-called patchwork quilt.

Mothers and daughters (often / entirely) sewed together. Also, whole towns (sometimes / very) joined together to work on quilts. ₃Over time, quilt designs became (already / increasingly) complex. They could take years to make.

The art of quilt making is still alive. It isn't about survival anymore. But it is still about family, tradition, and community.

NOTES quilt「キルト布団」 handicraft「手工芸」 practical「実用的な」 bedding「寝具」 layer「層」 filling「詰めもの」 well-off「裕福な」 scrap「切れ端」 complex「複雑な」 survival「生命の維持」

B **Comprehension** それぞれの文の内容が正しければ T(true) を、誤りであれば F(false) を○で囲みなさい。

1. The passage says quilts were expensive. 　　　　　　　T　F

2. Feathers might be found inside a quilt. 　　　　　　　T　F

3. These days, Americans still make quilts by hand. 　　　T　F

C **Translation** 前ページの英文の中で、下線が引かれている文を日本語に訳しなさい。

1. _____

2. _____

3. _____

--- **Reference Material** ---

頻度を表す副詞　List of Adverbs Expressing Frequency

always（いつも）	annually（毎年）	bimonthly（隔月に）
biweekly（隔週に）	daily（毎日）	frequently（ひんぱんに）
hourly（1時間ごとに）	monthly（毎月）	never（まったく…ない）
normally（通常は）	occasionally（たまに）	often（たびたび）
once（一度は）	rarely（めったに…しない）	seldom（めったに…ない）
sometimes（ときどき）	usually（たいてい）	yearly（年に1度、毎年）

時を表す副詞　List of Adverbs Expressing Time

ago（…前に）	already（すでに）	before（以前に）	belatedly（遅ればせながら）
early（早く）	ever（これまでに）	just（ちょうど）	late（遅く）
lately（最近）	later（あとで）	long（長く）	now（今）
recently（最近）	then（そのとき）	today（今日）	tomorrow（明日）
tonight（今夜）	since（それ以来）	soon（すぐに）	still（依然として）
yesterday（昨日）	yet（もう・まだ）		

場所を表す副詞　List of Adverbs Expressing Place

aboard（船内・機内・車内に）	abroad（海外へ）	across（横切って）
ahead（前方に）	around（周囲に）	away（離れて）
backward（うしろへ）	behind（後方に）	between（中間に）
beyond（向こうに）	down（下へ）	downstairs（下の階へ）
far（遠くへ）	forward（前へ）	here（ここで）
indoors（屋内で）	inside（中へ）	outside（外へ）
outdoors（屋外で）	over（上に）	there（あそこで）
up（上へ）	upstairs（上の階へ）	within（内側へ）

動詞＋不定詞　Following Certain Verbs

 Track 58

Bob remembered **to lock** the door.

Natalie wasn't asked **to clean** her desk.

Do I have **to replace** any major parts?

1. We need **to leave** in a few minutes.
   私たちは、あと数分で出発しなければならない。

2. They decided not **to buy** the house.
   彼らは、その家を購入しないことにした。

3. Does Melissa want **to be** on the team?
   メリッサはチームに加わりたいのですか。

> 「 to ＋動詞の原形 」という形の不定詞を「…すること」という意味で用いると、いくつかの動詞のうしろに置いて目的語として使うことができる。「…しないこと」と否定する場合は、not を不定詞の直前に置く。have は「to ＋動詞の原形」が付くと助動詞の働きをして「～しなければならない」と言う意味になる。

動詞＋目的語＋不定詞　Following Objects

 Track 59

Manuel taught her **to play** the guitar.

I didn't ask him **to dress** formally. It was his choice.

Do they want us **to turn off** our phones?

1. The store's owner is teaching me **to play** chess.
   その店の経営者は私にチェスのやり方を教えてくれている。

2. I didn't expect her **to come** to the party.
   私は、彼女がパーティーに来ることを期待していなかった。

3. Did you ask your nephew **to wash** the windows?
   あなたのおいに、窓掃除をするように頼みましたか。

> 動詞の中には、間接目的語と直接目的語という2つの目的語をとるものがある。そうした動詞の中には、to 不定詞を「…することを」という意味で使い、直接目的語にできるものがある。その場合、「主語 ＋ 動詞 ＋ 間接目的語（人）＋ 直接目的語（不定詞）」という形をとることが多い。

Track 60

She is afraid **to walk** down the dark street.

The young boy isn't eager **to rake up** the leaves.

Are you ready **to have** fun?

1. I'm glad **to know** you.
   あなたと知り合えてうれしいです。

2. The reservation was not easy **to make**.
   予約をするのは簡単ではなかった。

3. Were you excited **to meet** the singer?
   あなたは、その歌手に会えて興奮しましたか。

> いくつかの形容詞では直後に不定詞を続けて、「…をして…だ」と理由を示したり、「…をすることは…だ」という補足説明を加えたりすることができる。

Grammar Exercises

A （　）内の指示に従って、次の文を書き換えなさい。

[例]　Did he decide to go on the tour?　（肯定文に）

→ He decided to go on the tour.

1. They asked her to participate.　（疑問文に）

   _____

2. He is willing to share the reward.　（否定文に）

   _____

3. Allen doesn't want to buy a motorcycle.　（肯定文に）

   _____

4. Did he remind Hiroaki to bring a flashlight?　（肯定文に）

   _____

5. The poem is hard to understand.　（疑問文に）

   _____

93

B 次の文のあとに続く表現の記号を、空欄に書き入れなさい。

1. The bag is too heavy. She _____

2. It's cold. Can you ask him _____

3. It was an important game. The athletes _____

4. I know it's a big secret. I promise _____

5. Many deer live here. They're easy _____

(A) to close the window?

(B) not to tell anyone.

(C) to spot in the forest.

(D) were proud to win it.

(E) doesn't plan to buy it.

C 次の文を読み、その内容を正しく表しているものを A と B のどちらかから選びなさい。

1. Today, Mark has a big test. He didn't study much. He doubts he will get many questions right.

   (A) He expects to pass the test.

   (B) He is prepared to fail the test.

2. Jenny received a text message. It was an invitation to Evan's birthday party.

   (A) Jenny invited Evan to attend the party.

   (B) Evan invited Jenny to attend the party.

3. Their favorite band is coming to Tokyo. They slept outside to get tickets.

   (A) They are excited to see the band.

   (B) They were too scared to wait in line overnight.

Skill Building

A **Listening** 3つの文(A, B, C)を聞き、それぞれの内容と一致しているイラストの下にその記号を書きなさい。 🎧 Track 61

1. _____   2. _____   3. _____

| to see | to remind | to join | to found | to order |

Rick: I'm so hungry. Do you want 1( )?

Aiko: Let's wait a few more minutes. I invited Kurt 2( ) us for dinner.

Rick: Fantastic. It will be nice 3( ) him again. Is he still working at that film studio?

Aiko: No, he finally decided 4( ) his own company.

Rick: Good for him!

Aiko: Definitely. But now he's busier than ever. I have 5( ) him to get enough sleep and eat well.

質問の答えとして最も適切なものを選びなさい。

1. ( ) What does Rick want to do?
   A: Give Kurt a call   B: Invite a friend to dinner
   C: Order some food now   D: Watch a movie with Aiko

2. ( ) What do we learn about Kurt?
   A: He works at a film studio.
   B: He sleeps more than he should.
   C: Aiko cooks all of his meals.
   D: Kurt is a business owner.

C **Writing** 次の2つの文を、不定詞を使って1つの文にしなさい。その際は、( )内の語句を使うこと。

1. I forgot something. I didn't take out the garbage. (forgot, take out)

   I _____

2. The boss gave an order. Employees must work one weekend per month. (ordered, employees, work)

   The boss _____

3. They are happy. They live in a quiet neighborhood. (happy, live)

   They _____

Grammar Through Reading

A Reading Passage　（　　）内の単語を正しく並べ替え、空欄に書き込みなさい。

Sonia and Mario live in Rome. They are both successful businesspeople. Recently, they made a big decision. ₁They _____ _____ _____ (to / decided / follow) their dreams and leave the big city. The husband and wife _____ _____ _____ (move / to / plan) to the countryside and start a vineyard.

Mario grew up on a farm. As a child, his father _____ _____ _____ _____ (him / taught / grow / to) grapes and make wine. So he understands the process. Mario knows running the vineyard will be hard work. ₂But he is _____ _____ _____ _____ (to / excited / it / give) a try.

Sonia is also ready for the challenge. Plus, she's looking forward to the fresh country air. ₃But she's _____ _____ _____ _____ (say / to / sad / goodbye) to her best friend Nicola. Hopefully, Nicola can visit Sonia and Mario at the vineyard.

NOTES　countryside「田舎」　vineyard「ブドウ園」　process「手順、製法」　run「経営する、運営する」
ready for「…に対して覚悟ができている」　look forward to「…を期待する、…を楽しみに待つ」

B Comprehension　それぞれの文の内容が正しければ T(true) を、誤りであれば F(false) を○で囲みなさい。

1. Sonia and Mario are moving to a big city.　　T　F

2. Mario has some experience growing grapes.　　T　F

3. Sonia will probably miss Nicola.　　T　F

96

C **Translation** 前ページの英文の中で、下線が引かれている文を日本語に訳しなさい。

1. _____

2. _____

3. _____

Reference Material

> 不定詞のその他の用法　Other Uses of Infinitives

1. **To tell the truth**, I don't know.
   (本当のことを言うと、私は知らない)

2. We have enough money **to buy** it.
   (私たちには、それを買うのに十分なお金がある)

3. They waited in line **to buy** ice cream.
   (彼らはアイスクリームを買うために並んで待った)

4. The plan is **to leave** at noon.
   (その計画では、正午に出発するということだ)

5. To know her is **to like** her.
   (彼女を知ることは、好きになることになる)

6. It is impossible **to live** without electricity.
   (電気なしで暮らすことは不可能だ)

上記の用法についての解説：

(1) 文全体を修飾する慣用句として使われる独立不定詞。

(2) 「名詞＋不定詞」でその名詞を修飾し、「…するための…」「…するような…」という意味を表す形容詞的用法。

(3) 動詞を修飾して、「…するために」「…するように」という目的を表す副詞的用法。

(4) 名詞に相当する語句として、補語になる名詞的用法。

(5) 不定詞を文頭に置いて、主語として使う名詞的用法。

(6) It is ... to ... という構文で形式主語 it の内容を表す真主語。

16 動名詞 Gerunds

主語になる Subjects Track 62

Hiking is a good
way to get fresh air.

Biking in the rain
isn't very fun.

Is **painting** houses a good
way to make a living?

1. **Farming** is hard work.
   農作業はきつい仕事です。

2. **Spending** a lot of money isn't necessary.
   大金を使うことは必要ではない。

3. Is **losing** his job his biggest fear?
   失業することが、彼が一番心配していることですか。

> 動名詞は動詞の原形に -ing が付いたもので、名詞としての働きを持つ。「 …すること 」という意味になって主語として使うことができる。

動詞の目的語になる Following Certain Verbs Track 63

Today, the board discussed
expanding into Mexico.

He hasn't finished
building the fence.

How did you enjoy
traveling to Kenya?

1. We love **trying** food from other cultures.
   私たちは、異なる文化の食べ物を食べるのが大好きです。

2. I don't remember **meeting** her.
   彼女に会ったことは覚えていません。

3. Do you mind **waiting** for me outside?
   外で私を待っていてくれますか。

> 動名詞はいくつかの動詞の目的語として使い、「…することを」という意味を表すことができる。

Track 64

The boy is learning about **gardening**.

These scissors aren't the best for **cutting** cloth.

Is the speaker good at **explaining** his points?

1. By **studying** hard, you will improve.
   一生懸命に勉強することで、あなたの成績が上がるでしょう。

2. That artist isn't good at **drawing** hands.
   その画家は、人の手を描くのが上手ではない。

3. Are you interested in **sharing** a taxi?
   タクシーに相乗りする気はありますか。

> by -ing（…することによって）、at -ing（…することにおいて）、in -ing（…することについて）などのように、動名詞は前置詞の目的語として使うことができる。

Grammar Exercises

A 次の各文には、誤りが１つずつ含まれている。その誤りに線を引き、正しい形を空欄に書きなさい。

[例] Grandparents always enjoy see their grandchildren.
→ Grandparents always enjoy ~~see~~ their grandchildren. ___seeing___

1. Visit museums is a great way to learn about history. _____

2. The software is helpful for organize photos. _____

3. We discussed spend the holiday in Seoul. _____

4. How do you feel about train the new staff? _____

5. Being an adult means take responsibility for your actions. _____

6. Play the guitar helps me relax. _____

7. My best friend's hobby is draw birds. _____

8. By stretch before you run, you'll lower your injury risk. _____

B （　）内の正しい語句を選び、文を完成させなさい。

1. (Work / Working) in the entertainment industry is a lot of fun.

2. I'm sorry. I don't want (bothering / to bother / bother) you.

3. Thank you for (show / showing / to show) me the research center.

4. Do you remember (see / to see / seeing) the memo yesterday?

5. He can (meet / meeting / to meet) us at 4:30.

6. Our biggest challenge is (get / getting) enough signatures by Friday.

C 次の文が正しい文となるように、空欄に（　　）内の単語を原形のまま、または不定詞か動名詞に変えて入れなさい。

1. A: What do you usually _____ on the weekend? (do)

   B: Not much. I sometimes go bike _____ with my sister. (ride)

2. A: Did Hiroshi decide _____ at the animal shelter? (volunteer)

   B: He did. He really loves it.

3. A: This gadget is great for _____ pancake batter. (stir)

   B: You're right! It would also _____ perfect for cookie and cake mixes. (be)

Skill Building

A Listening　3つの文(A, B, C)を聞き、それぞれの内容と一致しているイラストの下にその記号を書きなさい。　🎧 Track 65

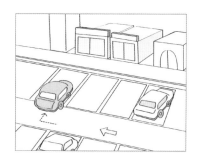  

1. _____　　　　2. _____　　　　3. _____

B **Speaking** 次の会話文を読み、以下のリストから適切な単語を選んで空欄を埋めなさい。

| using | training | sharing | learning | inviting |

Ron: Thank you again for ₁(   ) me over.

Lois: My pleasure. I love cooking big meals. But I prefer ₂(   ) them with friends.

Ron: Lucky for me. The pasta was delicious.

Lois: Thanks, Ron. The secret to making good sauce is ₃(   ) fresh ingredients. Are you interested in ₄(   ) to make it? I can teach you.

Ron: That sounds great. But most days, I barely have time to eat.

Lois: I understand. ₅(   ) for next month's big race must be hard. Well, it's time for dessert. I'll get the apple pie!

質問の答えとして最も適切なものを選びなさい。

1. (   ) How does Lois prefer eating big meals?
    A: By herself   B: With friends
    C: With her parents   D: With colleagues

2. (   ) What do we learn about Ron?
    A: He loves inviting friends over for meals.
    B: He is getting ready to take part in a race.
    C: He usually eats big dinners once a week.
    D: He liked the pie more than the pasta.

C **Writing** (   ) 内の語句を並べ替え、正しい文を作りなさい。

1. By (a discount / two boxes of pens, / you / buying / can get).

_____

2. Do (minutes / calling back / you mind / a few / in)?

_____

3. David's (is / passion / model trains / building).

_____

A **Reading Passage** 次の英文を読み、（　）内の正しいほうの単語を選びなさい。

Cosplay is popular among both women and men. Hobbyists hand-make costumes to look like comic, cartoon, TV, and movie characters. (Wearing / Putting) makeup creates an even more realistic look. Once the outfit is complete, cosplayers go to conventions. People gather around to take their photos. ₁Cosplayers enjoy (marking / posing) the same way as their characters.

A lot of hard work goes into the costumes. (Being / Sewing) the clothes takes many hours. ₂The best cosplayers are also experts at (making / pretending) accessories and props. The quality level is very high. Some of these creative masters are famous. They have many fans. For most people, though, it's just a fun and casual hobby. ₃Plus, (thinking / becoming) a cosplayer is a great way to flex your imagination.

NOTES cosplay「コスプレ」 hobbyist「趣味に熱中する人」 outfit「ひとそろいの衣装」 convention「集会」 gather around「集結する」 prop「小道具」 casual「気軽な」 flex「…を見せびらかす、試す」

B **Comprehension** それぞれの文の内容が正しければ T(true) を、誤りであれば F(false) を○で囲みなさい。

1. Generally, cosplayers don't like being photographed. 　　T　F

2. The best cosplayers make their own accessories. 　　T　F

3. Some cosplayers become famous, but most do not. 　　T　F

C **Translation**　前ページの英文の中で、下線が引かれている文を日本語に訳しなさい。

1. ＿＿＿＿＿＿＿＿＿＿＿＿＿＿＿＿＿＿＿＿＿＿＿＿＿＿＿＿＿＿＿＿＿＿＿＿

2. ＿＿＿＿＿＿＿＿＿＿＿＿＿＿＿＿＿＿＿＿＿＿＿＿＿＿＿＿＿＿＿＿＿＿＿＿

3. ＿＿＿＿＿＿＿＿＿＿＿＿＿＿＿＿＿＿＿＿＿＿＿＿＿＿＿＿＿＿＿＿＿＿＿＿

—— Reference Material ——

動名詞を目的語にとる動詞　List of Verbs Preceding Gerunds

1) 動名詞だけを目的語にできるもの

admit（…ということを認める）
consider（…することを検討する）
deny（…することを否定する）
dislike（…するのが嫌いだ）
escape（…することを免れる）
fancy（…するのを想像する）
give up（…するのをあきらめる）
mind（…するのをいやがる）
put off（…するのを先延ばしにする）
stop（…するのをやめる）

avoid（…することを避ける）
delay（…するのを遅らせる）
discuss（…することを議論する）
enjoy（…することを楽しむ）
excuse（…することを許す）
finish（…するのを終える）
involve（…することを伴う）
postpone（…するのを延期する）
quit（…するのをやめる）

2) 動名詞と不定詞の両方を目的語にできるもの

begin（…し始める）
continue（…し続ける）
like（…するのが好きである）
prefer（…するほうが好きである）

cease（…するのをやめる）
hate（…することを嫌う）
love（…するのが大好きである）
start（…し始める）

3) 動名詞と不定詞のどちらでも目的語にできるが、それぞれで意味が異なるもの

deserve -ing（…されるに値する）	deserve to...（…するに値する）
forget -ing（…したことを忘れている）	forget to...（…することを忘れている）
need -ing（…される必要がある）	need to...（…する必要がある）
regret -ing（…したことを後悔している）	regret to...（…することを残念に思う）
remember -ing（…したことを覚えている）	remember to...（忘れずに…する）
try -ing（試しに…してみる）	try to...（なんとか…してみようとする）
want -ing（…されなければならない）	want to...（…したいと思う）

17 接続詞 Conjunctions

複数の単語や語句を並べる　Compound Lists

 Track 66

She makes delicious cookies **and** pastries.

We can cross here **or** use the underpass.

The hotel's restaurant is costly **but** delicious.

1. Tom **and** Rachel work at a furniture store.
   トムとレイチェルは家具店で働いている。

2. With the set meal, you can have soup **or** salad.
   その定食では、スープかサラダを選べます。

3. We'll fly to Chicago on Friday **or** Saturday.
   私たちは金曜か土曜にシカゴに飛びます。

> いくつかの単語や語句を対等な関係で並べるときには、A and B（A と B）や、A or B（A か B）を使う。並べる要素が 3 つ以上ある場合は、それぞれをカンマで区切り、最後のものの前にだけ and や or を置く（A, B, C, and D）。

複数の文を並べる　Compound Sentences

 Track 67

Tomiko is studying business, **and** Paul is studying geology.

She wanted to shop at the store, **yet** it was closed.

There was supposed to be a game, **but** it started raining.

1. I'm 19, **and** my brother is 21.
   私は19歳で、兄は21歳だ。

2. We can walk, **or** we can catch a bus.
   私たちは歩いてもいいし、あるいはバスに乗ってもいい。

3. Hanna wanted to go out, **but** it was snowing.
   ハナは出かけたかったが、雪が降っていた。

> 複数の文も、and や or を使って並べることができる。and は、いくつかのことがらを並べる場合、or は、別の選択肢を示す場合に使われる。

The bears are **not only** cute **but also** well made.

Either today **or** tomorrow is fine for me to meet up.

I'd **rather** have a snack **than** a full meal.

1. **Both** jogging **and** swimming are great exercise.
   ジョギングと水泳のどちらも、とてもよい運動だ。

2. **Neither** the post office **nor** the bank is open.
   郵便局も銀行も開いていない。

3. **Not only** will the mayor join the parade, **but** he will **also** give a speech.
   市長はパレードに参加するだけでなく、スピーチもする予定だ。

> both A and B（A も B も）、either A or B（A か B のどちらか）、neither A nor B（A でも B でもない）、not only A but also B（A だけでなく B も）などのように、いくつかの語句が一対で使われて接続詞の働きをするものがある。なお、both A and B が主語のとき、動詞は A と B を合わせた数に対応し、それ以外の場合は、動詞は B の数に対応する。上の例文 3 のように、Not only A but also B の構文で A と B に文が使われる場合、A の文の主語と述語が倒置される。

Grammar Exercises

A （　）内の正しい語句を選び、文を完成させなさい。

1. For these sweaters, you can choose either red, black, (and / or / yet) white.

2. I'd be happy to help you move, (but / for / nor) I'm working all weekend.

3. (Either / Neither / Both) the pepper and the cinnamon are on the top shelf.

4. Sydney (for / and / nor) Paris both sound like amazing places to visit.

5. The heater is not only small (and / but / nor) also very warm.

6. We're new here, (or / also / and) we want to meet some neighbors.

7. Would you like milk (for / and / both) sugar with your coffee?

8. (Not / Neither / No) the salad nor the vegetable soup is fattening.

B 次の文のあとに続く表現の記号を、空欄に書き入れなさい。

1. I'd like to buy some pens, paper, _____

2. We can either watch a movie at home _____

3. Doris wants to get a cat, _____

4. These new phones are not only fast _____

5. The candle shop won't accept returns, _____

(A) but also stylish.

(B) nor will they let you exchange items.

(C) and a box of staples.

(D) or go to a theater.

(E) but her brother prefers dogs.

C 次の文の空欄に適切な接続詞を入れなさい。

1. A: What's the advantage of taking the train into the city?
   B: There are two. You can sleep on the train, _____ you don't have to look for a parking place.

2. A: Do you know where you're going to move yet?
   B: We're not sure. _____ we'll stay in the city, or we'll move somewhere near the ocean.

3. A: I love your backpack.
   B: Thanks! _____ _____ is it light, but it's also waterproof.

─────────── **Skill Building** ───────────

A Listening 3つの文(A, B, C)を聞き、それぞれの内容と一致しているイラストの下にその記号を書きなさい。 🎧 Track 69

1. _____   2. _____   3. _____

and	or	only	either	but

Aya:　To sell my jewelry online, do I need to build a website?

Leo:　I think you have two main choices. ₁(　　　　　) you can build a
website, ₂(　　　　　) you can use e-commerce sites to sell your jewelry.

Aya:　Hmm, I'm not sure about using those sites. It's more convenient,
　　　₃(　　　　　) I don't want to pay a lot.

Leo:　For some sites, you just pay a low monthly rate. Not ₄(　　　　　)
can you choose the store's name, but you can also design the page.

Aya:　That might work. Basically, I want to sell three types of things:
rings, necklaces, ₅(　　　　　) bracelets.

Leo:　Sounds simple enough. I'll be your first customer!

質問の答えとして最も適切なものを選びなさい。

1. (　　) What is Aya worried about?
　　　A: Spending a lot of money　　B: Shopping safely online
　　　C: Choosing a store name　　D: Finding customers

2. (　　) What does Leo say about e-commerce sites?
　　　A: They don't let people sell necklaces or bracelets.
　　　B: They are a little hard to use.
　　　C: They are the most convenient way to sell things.
　　　D: They let you design your page.

C **Writing**　以下に示す２つの文を、(　　) 内の語句を使って１つの文にしなさい。

1. He is an excellent soccer player. / He is also a great cook. (and)

_____

2. The tea isn't sweet. / The diet soda isn't sweet. (neither, nor)

_____

3. The class is interesting. / It's very popular. (not only, but also)

_____

Grammar Through Reading

Ⓐ Reading Passage　次の英文を読み、（　）内の正しいほうの語(句)を選びなさい。

For most of us, keeping in shape is a challenge. It's even more difficult for astronauts up in space. ₁<u>They have to pay special attention (both / either) to physical fitness (also / and) to nutrition.</u> Weightlessness is one major area of concern. It affects bone mass and causes muscles to atrophy. As a result, astronauts must exercise two hours a day.

Radiation is another problem. ₂<u>Special measures are needed (not only / neither) during spacewalks (but also / plus) inside the ship.</u> Astronauts' radiation levels are closely monitored during missions.

To keep their energy levels up, sleep is important. Astronauts try to get eight hours of sleep every day. Finally, they must have well-balanced diets. The good news is, before a mission, astronauts can choose their space meals. ₃<u>The meals may look boring, (or / but) some are delicious.</u>

NOTES　keep in shape「体型、体調を保つ」　astronaut「宇宙飛行士」　physical「肉体的な」
nutrition「栄養」　weightlessness「無重力状態」　mass「量」　atrophy「委縮する」
measure「対策」　boring「魅力がない」

Ⓑ Comprehension　それぞれの文の内容が正しければ T(true) を、誤りであれば
F(false) を○で囲みなさい。

1. In space, astronauts exercise every day to stay healthy.　　　　T　F

2. Astronauts only pay attention to radiation during spacewalks.　　T　F

3. During missions in space, astronauts can enjoy some excellent meals.　T　F

C Translation 前ページの英文の中で、下線が引かれている文を日本語に訳しなさい。

1. _____

2. _____

3. _____

Reference Material

等位接続詞　Summary Chart of Conjunctions

接続詞	意味	語(句)と語(句)を接続する	節と節を接続する
1. A and B	A および B	○	○
2. A or B	A または B	○	○
3. A but B	A しかし B	○	○
4. either A or B	A あるいは B	○	○
5. neither A nor B	A でも B でもない	○	○
6. not only A but also B	A だけでなく B も	○	○
7. both A and B	A も B も	○	
8. rather A than B	B よりもむしろ A	○	○
9. A, for B	A、なぜなら B だから		○

1. I love rings with stones like opals **and** rubies.

2. Would you like tea **or** coffee?

3. In the summer, Taiwan is hot **but** lively.

4. We'll take **either** a plane **or** a bullet train.

5. **Neither** dogs **nor** cats are allowed in the building.

6. Germany is **not only** beautiful **but also** rich in history.

7. **Both** silver **and** gold are considered precious metals.

8. I'd **rather** walk **than** take the bus.

9. Mateo stayed home, **for** he wasn't feeling well.

18 受動態　Passive Voice

能動態から受動態への書き換え　From Active to Passive Track 70

The sink **was fixed** by my nice neighbor.

This area **is enjoyed** by a lot of people in March.

Refreshments **will be provided** by a caterer.

1. Many people visit the temple. → The temple **is visited** by many people.
   多くの人たちがその寺院を訪れる。　　　　→ その寺院は多くの人たちに訪れられる。

2. Nobody stole the bicycle. → The bicycle **was not stolen**.
   誰もその自転車を盗んでいない。　　　　　→ その自転車は盗まれていない。

3. David will prepare the guest list. → The guest list **will be prepared** by David.
   デビッドが来客名簿を準備するでしょう。　→ 来客名簿はデビッドによって準備されるだろう。

> 動作を受けているものを主語にして文を作る場合には、受動態を使う。そのときの文は「動作を受けているもの＋ be 動詞＋動詞の過去分詞」という形をとる。否定文は be 動詞のあとに not を置いて作る。

助動詞のある受動態　Using Modals Track 71

Phones **must be turned off** before the movie starts.

The temperature **can be adjusted**.

Due to the heavy snowfall, the art festival **may not be held**.

1. The rule **might be changed**.
   その規則は変更されるかもしれない。

2. The sign **should be remade**.
   その看板は、作り直すべきだ。

3. These chairs **must not be moved**.
   それらの椅子は動かしてはいけません。

> 受動態の文で助動詞を使う場合、その助動詞は be 動詞の前に置き、be 動詞は原形のまま用いる。否定文では、not を助動詞と be 動詞の間に置く。

What **was stolen** by
the thief?

Will this item **be
sold** in the auction?

Can the bicycle **be
repaired**?

1. **Is** the club **recommended** by the guide book?
   そのクラブは、ガイドブックで勧められていますか。

2. **Will** the lecture **be given** by Dr. Grayson?
   その講義はグレイソン博士によって行われるのですか。

3. **Should** a public notice **be sent out**?
   公式な通知を出すべきでしょうか。

受動態の疑問文は、be 動詞を文頭に置いて作るが、助動詞を使う場合は、その助動詞を文頭に置く。

── **Grammar Exercises** ──

Ⓐ （　）内の指示に従って、次の文を書き換えなさい。

[例] A lot of children love the toy. （受動態の文に）
  → The toy is loved by a lot of children.

1. The entertainment will be provided by a band. （能動態の文に）

_____

2. The volume should be turned up. （否定文に）

_____

3. Their electricity was restored. （疑問文に）

_____

4. Are the doll eyes attached by a machine? （The doll eyes を主語にした平叙文に）

_____

5. Someone may repair the oven today. （受動態の文に）

_____

B 次の文を、例にならって受動態に変えなさい。

[例] Many people use that service. → That service _____ _____ by many people.

That service <u>is</u> <u>used</u> by many people.

1. Someone must clean up the park. → The park must _____ _____ up.

2. Did the guard set the alarm? → _____ the alarm _____ by the guard?

3. Nobody changed the code. → The code _____ _____ _____.

C 次の文を読み、その内容を正しく表しているものをAとBのどちらかから選びなさい。

1. Mr. Kimura arrived at work at 8:15. In the parking lot, he saw a car with a broken window. He wrote down the license plate and told a security guard.

   (A) The window was broken by Mr. Kimura.

   (B) The broken window was reported by Mr. Kimura.

2. Diego and Luna went to a travel agency. They asked about vacations to Canada. An agent gave them details about several choices.

   (A) The details were provided by the travel agent.

   (B) The vacation was booked by the couple online.

3. Kaoru is selling her bike. She listed it online at a price of 10,000 yen. Someone offered her 6,000 yen. Kaoru feels that price is too low.

   (A) The offer will be accepted by Kaoru.

   (B) The offer will be rejected by Kaoru.

--- **Skill Building** ---

A **Listening** 3つの文(A, B, C)を聞き、それぞれの内容と一致しているイラストの下にその記号を書きなさい。 🎧 Track 73

1. _____ 2. _____ 3. _____

was shot	were entered	was started	was awarded	were taken

Daniel: The photography club ₁(   ) three years ago by a group of students.

Yukiko: Is this the club's work along the walls?

Daniel: Yes, all the photos ₂(   ) by our members. A few ₃(   ) into competitions.

Yukiko: Did they win any prizes?

Daniel: Yes, some. The one with the blue ribbon ₄(   ) first prize in a big contest.

Yukiko: Nice! Let me see the description. Oh, it ₅(   ) with a Canon. It's the same camera that I use.

質問の答えとして最も適切なものを選びなさい。

1. (   ) What can be seen along the walls?
　　A: Lists of competitions　　B: Photos taken by club members
　　C: Ads for different cameras　　D: Drawings done by Daniel

2. (   ) What does Yukiko say about the winning photo?
　　A: The photo was taken by her friend.
　　B: She owns the type of camera used to take the photo.
　　C: The photo and description appeared in a magazine.
　　D: She loves the photo's blue colors.

C Writing (   ) 内の語句を並べ替え、正しい文を作りなさい。

1. The (by many / worn / hats / young people / are).

_____

2. That form (be / in / need to / filled / doesn't).

_____

3. Will (delayed / flight / be / to Hanoi / our)?

_____

Grammar Through Reading

A Reading Passage （　）内の動詞を、時制に注意して受動態に変えなさい。

In the center of Bangkok, the capital of Thailand, is a beautiful site: the Grand Palace. It _____ _____ (visit) by many tourists, and for good reason. The palace is a classical, peaceful complex in a busy, dynamic city.

₁The Grand Palace _____ _____ (complete) in 1782. For 150 years, it was both the home of the king and the center of Thailand's government. The king's home and the government offices _____ _____ (relocate) about a hundred years ago. However, the palace is still used on special occasions.

₂Some of the buildings can _____ _____ (tour) by visitors. That includes the Temple of the Emerald Buddha. Inside is a small emerald statue. ₃It _____ _____ (make) in the 14th century. The temple and other palace buildings represent some of Asia's finest architecture.

NOTES　Grand Palace「王宮」 complex「建築物の集合体」 complete「完成する」
relocate「移転する」 temple「寺院」 statue「立像」 represent「代表する」 architecture「建築物」

B Comprehension　それぞれの文の内容が正しければ T(true) を、誤りであれば F(false) を○で囲みなさい。

1. In Bangkok, the Grand Palace is popular with visitors.　　　　T　F

2. The Grand Palace was built 150 years ago.　　　　T　F

3. There is a statue inside the Temple of the Emerald Buddha.　　　T　F

114

C **Translation** 前ページの英文の中で、下線が引かれている文を日本語に訳しなさい。

1. _____

2. _____

3. _____

―――――――――――― **Reference Material** ――――――――――――

よく使われる受動態の表現　Commonly Used Passive Expressions

感覚や感情を表す場合に、受動態が使われる場合が多い。

amazed（びっくりする）	ashamed（恥ずかしく思う）	bored（退屈する）
confused（混乱する）	delighted（大喜びする）	depressed（落胆する）
disappointed（失望する）	excited（興奮する）	frightened（怖がる）
interested（興味を持つ）	obliged（感謝している）	offended（気を悪くする）
pleased（喜ぶ）	satisfied（満足する）	surprised（驚く）
tired（疲れている）	worried（心配している）	shocked（ショックを受ける）
terrified（ぞっとする）		

経歴・人間関係を表すもの。

born（生まれる）	raised / reared（育てられる）	educated（教育を受ける）
employed（雇われる）	promoted（昇進する）	fired / laid off（解雇される）
engaged（婚約する・従事する）	married（結婚する）	divorced（離婚する）
separated（別居する）	reunited（仲直りする）	

ニュース報道などで、行為者が不明なときや行為者を曖昧にしたいとき、行為者が自明なとき、客観性を持たせたいとき、被害を強調するときなどに受動態がよく使われる。

delayed（遅れる）	damaged（破壊される）	crowded（混雑している）
burned（焼ける）	stolen（盗まれる）	robbed（強盗に遭う）
attacked（攻撃される）	injured（けがをする）	wounded（傷を負う）
hospitalized（入院する）	killed（死ぬ）	murdered（殺害される）
involved（関わる）	arrested（逮捕される）	sued（訴えられる）
convicted（有罪になる）	sentenced（判決を言い渡される）	imprisoned（収監される）
defeated（敗北する）	rescued（救出される）	believed（信じられている）

よく使われる接頭辞　Common Prefixes

Track 74

The house is **sur**rounded by trees.

They haven't finished **pre**paring the meeting room.

Should he **re**place the old bike tires?

1. I work for a big **auto**mobile parts maker.
   私は大手の自動車部品メーカーに勤めています。

2. My sister isn't interested in **com**puters.
   私の妹はコンピューターに興味がありません。

3. Did you **pre**order the new game?
   あなたはその新作ゲームの事前予約をしましたか。

> 英語には、単語の前に付けられて、元の意味を補ったり変えたりする接頭辞がいくつかある。たとえば、auto（自ら）が mobile（移動する）と組み合わされて automobile（自動車）という意味になる。よく使われる接頭辞の意味を知っていると、初めて見る単語でもその意味を推測できることがある。

よく使われる語根　Common Roots

Track 75

The price de**pend**s on the weight.

He doesn't usually play this **ver**sion of the game.

How many images does the **vis**ual dictionary have?

1. Our com**mand**er told us to stay here.
   司令官は私たちに、この場にとどまるように言った。

2. There isn't a public tele**phon**e in the building.
   その建物内には公衆電話がありません。

3. What does the factory pro**duc**e?
   その工場は何を生産していますか。

> 単語の基本的な意味を表す部分を「語根」といい、さまざまな接頭辞や接尾辞と組み合わされて、別の単語が作られる。たとえば、bio（生、生命）という語根を持つ単語に、biology（生物学）や biography（伝記）、antibiotic（抗生物質）などがある。

Next, I add sugar to
sweet**en** the pudding.

The outfit may not be
suit**able** for the party.

Is he a professional
pian**ist**?

動詞をつくる　(-ate, -en, -fy)

1. They should short**en** the movie by 20 minutes.
   その映画は20分短くすべきだ。

形容詞をつくる　(-able, -ful, -less)

2. The house isn't beauti**ful**, but it is big.
   その家は美しくないけれど広い。

名詞をつくる　(-er, -ion, -ist)

3. What's the solut**ion** to the problem?
   その問題の解決策は、どのようなものですか。

語の末尾に付けて、意味を加えたり、品詞を変化させたりする接尾辞がいくつかある。

Grammar Exercises

A　（　）内の正しい語を選び、文を完成させなさい。

1. Arthur isn't afraid of anything. He is (fearing / fearless / fearful).

2. We are a leading (production / produce / producer) of light bulbs.

3. Nell is a (perfectionist / perfectly / perfect). Everything must be exactly right.

4. The pen is (refill / refillable / refilling). It's easy to add more ink.

5. With this new information, we'll need to (modify / modifier / modification)
   the report.

6. Our (supply / supplies / supplier) is great. He's never late with shipments.

7. I'm sorry for not being (cared / careful / careless). I left the sink running.

8. The government (regulations / regulates / regulating) factories. The air
   quality must meet a certain standard.

B 次の単語の意味を (A) ～ (E) の中から選び、その記号を空欄に書きなさい。

1. _____ prediction   (A) plentiful / having a lot of something

2. _____ induce   (B) make longer

3. _____ bountiful   (C) another possibility or choice

4. _____ alternative   (D) a guess about something before it happens

5. _____ lengthen   (E) make happen / get someone to do something

C （　　）内の単語を正しい形に変えて空欄に入れなさい。

1. A: What a great _____! (perform)

   B: I agree. It was a fantastic show.

2. A: What's the _____ between this city and the ocean? (distant)

   B: About 50 kilometers. Some _____ have small boats. (reside)
   They take them out to the ocean every month or so.

3. A: I don't understand the _____ of this TV show. (attract)

   B: I really like it. All the _____ are excellent, and so is the
   director. (act)

─────────── **Skill Building** ───────────

A **Listening**   3つの文(A, B, C)を聞き、それぞれの内容と一致しているイラストの
下にその記号を書きなさい。　🎧 Track 77

1. _____   2. _____   3. _____

| adventures | prefer | transportation | courage | independent |

Celine: I can't believe you're traveling to Chile alone. That takes a lot of
₁(   ).

Rico: Oh, I don't know. There are lots of ₂(   ) travelers in Chile.

Celine: I ₃(   ) traveling with a tour group. That way I don't need
to worry about ₄(   ). I'm bad with maps and directions.

Rico: Tours do make things easier. But then you miss out on a lot.

Celine: Like what?

Rico: Like meeting new people and having ₅(   ). When you
travel alone, anything can happen!

質問の答えとして最も適切なものを選びなさい。

1. (   ) How does Rico prefer to travel?
    A: With a friend   B: With a tour group
    C: With his family   D: By himself

2. (   ) What problem does Celine have when traveling?
    A: She doesn't know any languages besides English.
    B: She isn't good at using maps.
    C: She has trouble making friends.
    D: She has a hard time choosing good tour guides.

C **Writing** 次の各文で、下線が付けられている単語を（　　）内の指示に従って
変え、同じ意味となる文を作りなさい。

1. The man has a lot of <u>strength</u>. （名詞から形容詞に）

   He   very

2. Sally <u>advised</u> me about a personal matter. （動詞から名詞に）

   She gave   some good

3. We need to make the table <u>longer</u>. （形容詞から動詞に）

   We need to

A **Reading Passage** 次の英文を読み、( ) 内の正しいほうの単語を選びなさい。

Nikola Tesla was one of history's greatest minds. ₁His numerous (inventors / inventions) changed the world. Tesla was born in Croatia in 1856. ₂He studied (engineer / engineering) in Austria. As a young man, he was already doing (important / importance) work in the field. Early on, he developed a way to use alternating current (AC) electricity.

In 1884, Tesla moved to the USA. He briefly worked for Thomas Edison. The next year, Tesla sold his AC system patent to George Westinghouse.

₃Over the (followed / following) decades, Tesla invented many other things. One was the Tesla coil in 1891. More than 100 years later, these coils are still found in many radios and televisions. Speaking of radios, that was yet another creation of this (amazed / amazing) genius.

NOTES　**Nikola Tesla**「クロアチア生まれの米国の発明家」 **mind**「人物、人間」
numerous「非常に多くの」 **alternating current**「交流」 **briefly**「しばらくの間」
patent「特許」 **decade**「10 年間」 **coil**「変圧器」 **genius**「天才」

B **Comprehension** それぞれの文の内容が正しければ T(true) を、誤りであれば F(false) を○で囲みなさい。

1. Nikola Tesla was born in America. 　　　　　　　　　　　T　F

2. Tesla sold his AC system patent before his 40th birthday. 　T　F

3. Some of Tesla's inventions are still used. 　　　　　　　　T　F

C Translation　前ページの英文の中で、下線が引かれている文を日本語に訳しなさい。

1. _____

2. _____

3. _____

Reference Material

よく使われる接頭辞　Chart of Common Prefixes

接頭辞	意味	例
a-	非・無	anonymous, apathy
bi-	二つ・両方	bicycle, biannual
co-	共に	colleague, cooperate
kilo-	千	kilogram, kilometer
micro-	微少の	microscope, microphone
multi-	複数の・多様な	multiple, multitask
pre-	事前の	predate, prepare
re-	再び	replace, redo
sur-	超えて	surround, surface
tele-	遠くの	telephone, telegram

よく使われる語根　Chart of Common Roots

語根	意味	例
bio	生命	biology, biography
dict	言葉	dictation, predict
dom	家	domestic, domicile
duc / duct	導く	conduct, introduce
mand	命令	command, demand
nat	誕生	nature, innate
pend / pens	ぶら下がる	pending, expensive
phon	音	microphone, phonetic
rupt	破る	rupture, disrupt
sens / sent	感じる	sensitive, consent
vers / vert	向く	version, convert
vid / vis	見る	video, visual

20 形容詞節 Adjective Clauses

  Track 78

The man **who designed this building** is famous.

The person **that bought the painting** is not from this area.

Is Liza the director **who won a bunch of awards**?

1. Mr. Tanaka is the man **who taught me to paint**.
   タナカ先生は、私に絵の描き方を教えてくれた人です。

2. The manager **with whom you should speak** is not here.
   あなたが話をすべき部長は、ここにはいません。

3. Is that the artist **whose work you admire**?
   あの人が、あなたの憧れている画家ですか。

> 人を表す名詞や代名詞があるとき、そのうしろに who、that、whom、whose などの語句を続けて形容詞節を作り、その人についての説明文を加えることができる。

場所の説明を加える　Places Track 79

Is this the place **where you and Jack usually go**?

The farm **which will host the celebration** isn't near any highways.

Is this the restaurant **that serves free desserts**?

1. It's the town **where I was born**.
   そこが私の生まれた町です。

2. This isn't the aquarium **which we read about**.
   ここは、私たちが読んで知った水族館ではありません。

3. Was the place **that you visited** in the mountains?
   あなたが訪れた場所は山の中にあったのですか。

> 場所を示す名詞があるとき、うしろに where や which、that などの語句を置いて形容詞節を作り、その場所についての説明文を加えることができる。

Track 80

This is the
bus **that goes
downtown**.

Iguanas aren't the type
of pet **which many
people want to raise**.

Is this the book **that
you were looking
for**?

1. The cat **which jumped on the table** is named Mickey.
   テーブルの上に飛び乗ってきたネコは、ミッキーという名です。

2. That isn't the bird species **that I referred to**.
   それは私の言っていた鳥類ではありません。

3. Do you sell any computer batteries **which last 10 hours**?
   10時間使えるコンピューター用バッテリーは売っていますか。

動物や物を表す名詞の場合は、うしろに which または that を置いて、説明文を加えることができる。

Grammar Exercises

A　（　）内の指示に従って、次の文を書き換えなさい。

[例] It is the town where the movie was filmed.　（否定文に）

　　→ It is not the town where the movie was filmed.

1. He is the person who leads the group.　（疑問文に）

　_____

2. Are these the shells which she found at the beach?　（平叙文に）

　_____

3. The bus that goes to the convention center is comfortable.　（否定文に）

　_____

4. It's not the shop whose owner just turned 90.　（肯定文に）

　_____

5. The place where we buy bagels is closed on Sundays.　（疑問文に）

　_____

B （　）内の正しい語を選び、文を完成させなさい。

1. Let me show you some dresses (which / who) we just got in.

2. The man (who / whom) lives across the street is a lawyer.

3. Do you know any places (where / which) I can get handmade soap?

4. This information is for travelers (that / whose) visa is about to expire.

5. The person to (whom / where) the flowers were sent was not home.

C 次の文の空欄に who、whom、which、whose、where のいずれかを補いなさい。

1. A: Is Detroit the city _____ you two met?
   B: Actually, no. We met in San Francisco. I attended a conference _____ Mary organized.

2. A: The company is looking for someone _____ speaks Arabic.
   B: I studied Arabic for three years. Maybe I should apply for the job.

3. A: Elizabeth Barrett Browning is someone _____ writing I admire.
   B: I recently read something which you might already know. The person for _____ she wrote many poems was her husband, Robert.

--- **Skill Building** ---

A **Listening**　3つの文(A, B, C)を聞き、それぞれの内容と一致しているイラストの下にその記号を書きなさい。 🎧 Track 81

1. _____　　　2. _____　　　3. _____

| where | whom | which | whose | who |

Ellen: Your ninth move was fantastic! I think it's the one ₁(   ) won you the match.

Pedro: Thanks. Did I ever tell you about the man ₂(   ) taught me to play chess?

Ellen: I don't think so.

Pedro: He's the one to ₃(   ) I owe everything. His name is Alex. He went to a university ₄(   ) everybody played chess.

Ellen: Interesting. Is he the person ₅(   ) website you told me about?

Pedro: Right, same guy. The site has some of his best strategies.

質問の答えとして最も適切なものを選びなさい。

1. (   ) What do we learn about Pedro's chess match?
    A: Ellen's coaching was important to Pedro's success.
    B: Alex played well, but Pedro played even better.
    C: The match was held at a famous university.
    D: His ninth move gave him a good chance to win.

2. (   ) How can someone learn about Alex's chess strategies?
    A: By visiting his website   B: By attending his class
    C: By reading his book   D: By playing a lot of matches

C **Writing** (   ) 内の語句を並べ替え、正しい文を作りなさい。

1. The book (has / that / truly amazing / some photos / are).

_____

2. The Ganges (which provides / many people / a river / water to / is).

_____

3. Beethoven is (music / widely loved / a composer / is / whose).

_____

A **Reading Passage** 次の英文を読み、（　）内の正しいほうの単語を選びなさい。

₁Balancing private and professional lives is a challenge (where / whose / which) many people face. Some people work at companies (where / that / who) everyone works long hours. Others must hold more than one job to pay the bills. ₂Then there are people (whom / where / who) simply love to work. They are ambitious and want to make a mark in their fields.

Other people take the opposite path. They devote themselves to their families. ₃Of course, that is easier in families in (whose / which / that) one spouse has a good income. Perhaps the hardest path is working while raising a family. Yet many people do just that.

In the 21st century, it's hard to say which lifestyle is best. The world is full of people for (whom / which / whose) every day is both a challenge and a reward.

NOTES professional「職業の」 bill「勘定、請求金額」 ambitious「野心がある」 make a mark「成功する、有名になる」 opposite「逆の」 devote oneself to ...「…に専念する」 spouse「配偶者」 reward「報い、報酬」

B **Comprehension** それぞれの文の内容が正しければ T(true) を、誤りであれば F(false) を○で囲みなさい。

1. The article says some people enjoy working.　　T　F

2. Focusing on both work and family is the hardest lifestyle.　　T　F

3. These days, everyone agrees on the same lifestyle path.　　T　F

C **Translation**　前ページの英文の中で、下線が引かれている文を日本語に訳しなさい。

1. _____

2. _____

3. _____

Reference Material

前置詞＋関係代名詞　Preposition + Relative Pronoun

1. She is someone **in whom** I have complete confidence.

2. It isn't a subject **about which** I'm very knowledgeable.

3. Is that a purchase **for which** we need a manager's approval?

関係代名詞の whom や which が前置詞の目的語となる場合、前置詞は関係代名詞の前に置かれることがある。その場合はやや改まった言い方になる。ただし、関係代名詞の that の場合は、前置詞がその前に置かれることはない。

時間＋ when / that　Time + when / that...

1. That was **a time when** we were all working nights and weekends.

2. Here's a photo of **the day that** our son graduated from college.

3. Fall is **the season when** we spend the most time outdoors.

特定の日時や期間についての説明を加える場合は、その語句を先行詞として関係副詞の when で始まる節を続ける。when は that で代用することもでき、省略される場合もある。

理由＋ why　Reason (+ why)...

1. Those items break easily. That's the **reason why** they're in a glass case.

2. I don't understand the **reason why** we're not allowed to sit here.

3. Can you please tell me the **reason** this gate is locked?

reason「理由」を先行詞にして、その理由を説明する場合は、関係副詞の why で始まる節を続ける。3. の文のように why が省略されることもある。また、the reason が省略されて why だけが残る場合もある（2. の文では the reason を省略できる）。

21 副詞節 Adverb Clauses

Danica will go out **after the weather improves**.

Once she felt better, Alice took a short swim.

While Maya stacked the fruit, Tim brought more out.

1. I need to finish my homework **before I go anywhere**.
   私は出かける前に、宿題を終えなければならない。

2. We will call you **after we arrive**.
   私たちが到着したら、あなたに電話をかけます。

3. **When it's time to leave**, I'll let you know.
   出発する時間になったら、あなたに知らせます。

> 時間を表す接続詞のあとに主語と動詞を続けて、時を表す副詞節を作ることができる。未来のことでも副詞節の中の動詞は現在形になることに注意。

原因・理由を表す　Causal Relationships Track 83

Because there is only one bank machine, there is a line to use it.

The store will gift wrap the shirt **since it is a present**.

As he had nothing else to do, he washed his car.

1. **As it's raining**, we should cancel the game.
   雨が降っているので、試合は中止すべきです。

2. **Because the restaurant was full**, we went back home and ate.
   そのレストランが満席だったので、私たちは自宅に戻って食事をした。

3. I will attend the conference **since it sounds interesting**.
   おもしろそうなので、私はその会議に出席するつもりです。

> あるできごとの原因や理由を表すため、as や because、since などの接続詞を使って「…だから」「…のため」という意味の副詞節を作ることができる。

Track 84

She will buy the ring
**even though it is
expensive.**

**Although the lake
was a little crowded,**
we rented a boat.

Mike is a big soccer fan,
**whereas his best friend
Annie loves basketball**.

1. **Although it's snowing,** I still want to go jogging.
   雪が降っているけれど、それでも私はジョギングに出かけたい。

2. **Whereas Kumiko will stay home,** her brother will go camping.
   クミコは家にいる予定だが、彼女の兄はキャンプに出かけるつもりだ。

3. We'll take the back roads **even though it will take longer**.
   時間は余計にかかるけれど、私たちは裏道を進むつもりです。

> although や even though、whereas など、ことがらを対比させる接続詞を使って、「…だけれども」「…にもかかわらず」という意味の副詞節を作ることができる。

Grammar Exercises

A　次の文を読み、A と B のうち内容が正しいほうを選びなさい。

1. Nobuyuki talked on the phone for 15 minutes. Then he put on his coat. Finally, he walked to the bus station to meet his friend.

   (A) Before Nobuyuki met his friend, he talked on the phone.

   (B) Nobuyuki talked on the phone as he walked to the bus station.

2. At the stadium, Ivan asked about opening day tickets. They were all sold out. He decided to look for tickets on the Internet.

   (A) Ivan bought tickets at the stadium since they were available there.

   (B) As the stadium was out of tickets, Ivan tried to get some online.

3. We warned Junko about buying stock in the hi-tech company. She bought some stock anyway. A month later, the company went out of business.

   (A) After people warned her, Junko stayed away from the stock.

   (B) Junko bought the stock even though people advised her not to.

B 次の文のあとに続く表現の記号を、空欄に書き入れなさい。

1. Once it was warm enough, _____

2. As we're buying a house, _____

3. They leave the heater on all night _____

4. I will book the plane ticket _____

5. Because there were no seats, _____

(A) we applied for a loan.

(B) after the trip dates are set.

(C) he had to stand the whole way.

(D) Sara went out for a walk.

(E) even though energy costs are high.

C （　）内の正しい語を選び、文を完成させなさい。

1. (Once / Although) the economy is bad, they want to invest in real estate.

2. The hillside is beautiful (after / even though) the flowers bloom.

3. (Now that / Whereas) he has his own studio, the photographer can start looking for clients.

4. It isn't safe to look at your phone (before / while) you drive.

5. They need to find a new dentist (since / when) their current one is retiring.

6. (Though / After) the road work is completed, traffic will be smoother.

7. The meeting was extended (because / even though) they were not finished discussing everything.

8. (When / While) the printer stopped working, I took it back to the shop.

Skill Building

A **Listening**　3つの文(A, B, C)を聞き、それぞれの内容と一致しているイラストの下にその記号を書きなさい。　🎧 Track 85

1. _____　　　　2. _____　　　　3. _____

B **Speaking** 次の会話文を読み、以下のリストから適切な語 (句) を選んで空欄を埋めなさい。

| even though | before | now that | because | after |

Lori: Why did you build a fence in front of your house?

Steve: I did it ₁( ) the neighbor's dog was coming over. It was ruining our garden.

Lori: That's terrible. Did you try talking with your neighbor?

Steve: Sure. But a few weeks ₂( ) I talked to him, the problem started up again. Anyway, it's OK. ₃( ) we have a fence, we're going to plant a lot more flowers.

Lori: Now that's a positive attitude! I'd love to plant some flowers in front of my house. ₄( ) our yard is small, it might be fun.

Steve: ₅( ) you plant anything, talk to my wife. She's an expert.

質問の答えとして最も適切なものを選びなさい。

1. ( ) What problem did Steve have before building the fence?
   A: Neighbors making noise　　B: Bikers riding over the garden
   C: Insects eating his flowers　　D: An animal causing trouble

2. ( ) What does Lori say about her house?
   A: There are too many dogs in the area.
   B: She has plenty of room to plant many flowers.
   C: If she starts a garden, it will need to be small.
   D: It's in the same city as Steve's house.

C **Writing** 以下に示す２つの文を、( ) 内の語句を使って１つの文にしなさい。

1. Mr. Miyagi will repair the sink. / Then he will repair the dishwasher. (After)

   _____

2. The river is off-limits to swimmers. / The reason is it is polluted. (because)

   _____

3. Sharks are widely feared. / They are important to the environment. (Whereas)

   _____

A **Reading Passage**　次の英文を読み、（　）内の正しいほうの語(句)を選びなさい。

A currency's strength or weakness can heavily impact a country's economy. ₁That's especially true (now that / before) all our economies are linked. (Though / When) a currency becomes too strong, it makes exports less competitive. The situation also hurts the profits of exporting companies. (Because / Whereas) these drawbacks are serious, there are bright spots. For instance, a strong currency makes imports like energy cheaper.

On the other side of the issue, a weak currency can boost exports. ₂(After / Even though) a currency falls, it can also help the local tourism sector. However, the situation creates the danger of higher inflation.

In general, governments prefer a weaker currency, mostly for the sake of trade. Still, there is one key point to consider. ₃(As / Although) many governments hate to see their currencies rise, there's usually little they can do about it.

NOTES　currency「通貨」 impact「影響を及ぼす」 competitive「競争力がある」 drawback「不利益」 energy「エネルギー源」 on the other side of ...「…のもう一方の側では」 boost「増やす」 tourism「観光業」 sector「部門」 for the sake of ...「…のために」

B **Comprehension**　それぞれの文の内容が正しければ T(true) を、誤りであれば F(false) を○で囲みなさい。

1. The profits of exporting companies are hurt by a strong currency.　　T　F

2. Weak currencies can be a big help to local tourism.　　T　F

3. It's easy for governments to affect a currency's strength or weakness.　　T　F

C **Translation** 　前ページの英文の中で、下線が引かれている文を日本語に訳しなさい。

1. _____

2. _____

3. _____

Reference Material

副詞節を導く接続詞　Chart of Adverb Clause Types

接続詞	意味
A that B	1) B するように A　2) B なので A　3) A の結果 B
A whether B	B かどうかは A
A if B	1) B かどうかは A　2) もし B なら A
A unless B	もし B でなければ A
A when B	B のとき A
A as B	1) B のとき A　2) B なので A
A whenever B	B のときはいつでも A
A as long (far) as B	B であるかぎり A
A while B	1) B の一方で A　2) B の間は A
A whereas B	B なのに A
A until (till) B	B するまで A
A since B	1) B 以来 A　2) B なので A
A because B	B なので A
A though (although) B	B だけれども A
A even though (even if) B	たとえ B でも A
A as though (as if) B	まるで B のように A
A before B	B の前に A
A after B	B のあとに A
A as soon as B	B するとすぐに A
A once B	いったん B すれば A
A lest B	B だといけないから A
A where B	B のところに A
A so (in order) that B	B するように A

22 仮定法 Conditionals

可能性の高いことを仮定する　Real / Possible Situations Track 86

If my stylist **is** available, I **will get** a haircut tomorrow.

He **might take** an express train **if there is** one leaving soon.

If she **finishes** work by 5:30, she **will go** jogging.

1. **If** I **have** time, I **bake** cookies on Sundays.（時間があれば）

   もし時間があれば、私は日曜日にクッキーを焼きます。

2. **If** the weather **is** bad, we **will not go** hiking.（天気が悪ければ）

   天気が悪ければ、私たちはハイキングに行かないつもりです。

3. We **will visit** the studio **if** we **have** a chance.（チャンスがあれば）

   チャンスがあれば、私たちはそのスタジオを訪ねるでしょう。

4. I **may pick up** some milk **if** the grocery store **is** open.（店が開いていれば）

   その食料品店が開いていれば、牛乳を買うかもしれません。

> 「もし…ならば…する」というように、ある条件とその結果を単純に述べる場合は、「If ＋主語＋動詞の現在形、主語＋（助動詞）＋動詞の原形」という構文が使われる。

事実に反すること、可能性の低いことを仮定する　Unreal / Impossible Situations Track 87

They **would take** a ferry across the lake **if** the service **were offered**.

If we **had** more space, we **could fit** more desks in here.

If their star player **had not been** hurt, the team **might have won** more games.

1. Tammy **would tell** you **if** she **knew**.（彼女は知らない）

   もしタミーが知っていたら、あなたに教えるでしょう。

2. I **would not take** the job **if I were** you. （私はあなたではない）

   私があなただったら、その仕事には就かないでしょう。

3. **If** it **were** possible, we **would travel** abroad every year. （その可能性は低い）

   もしできることなら、私たちは毎年、海外旅行に出かけるのに。

4. **If** you **had gone** to the party, you **could have met** Gary. （あなたはパーティーに行かなかった）

   もしあなたがそのパーティーに行っていたら、ギャリーに会えたのに。

現在の事実に反することを仮定して、「もし…ならば…するのに」と言うときは、if 節の中の時制を過去にし、結論部分は「主語＋ would (could, might, should) ＋動詞の原形」を使って表現する。このとき、if 節の中に be 動詞が使われていたら、主語が I や it、he、her であっても were が使われることが多い。また、過去の事実に反することを仮定して、「もし…だったら…したのに」と言うときは、if 節の中の時制を過去完了にし、結論部分は「主語＋ would (could, might, should) ＋ have ＋動詞の過去完了形」を使う。

Grammar Exercises

Ⓐ　（　）内の正しい語を選び、文を完成させなさい。

1. They will visit their cousin if there (was / is) time.

2. If I (were / was) you, I would listen to Mr. Lin's advice.

3. If we decide to remodel the room, we (will / would) hire an interior decorator.

4. If they (have / had) provided food, the reception would have been better.

5. We may move the tournament to a larger location if more people (sign / signed) up.

6. I would (transfer / have transfer) to another department if I had a choice.

7. If the server (goes / went) down, our IT expert can fix it.

8. If we had known how long the trip was, we (will / would) not have driven to the botanical gardens.

B 次の文のあとに続く表現の記号を、空欄に書き入れなさい。

1. If the spa offers the service, _____

   (A) I would let you use it.

2. He would go scuba diving _____

   (B) if enough students want to take them.

3. We would have invited you _____

   (C) if he didn't have to work.

4. They may offer drama classes _____

   (D) if we had known you liked river rafting.

5. If I didn't need my car today, _____

   (E) she will get a massage.

C 次の文を読み、A と B のうち内容が正しいほうを選びなさい。

1. If Gregory had the power, he would change the policy.

   (A) Gregory doesn't want to change the policy.

   (B) Gregory doesn't have the power to change the policy.

2. They will plant some orange trees if there is room on the property.

   (A) They may plant some orange trees.

   (B) There is definitely not enough room for orange trees.

3. If the trail had not been closed, they would have hiked to the waterfall.

   (A) It was possible to hike to the waterfall, but they didn't do it.

   (B) They were not able to visit the waterfall.

Skill Building

A **Listening** 3つの文(A, B, C)を聞き、それぞれの内容と一致しているイラストの下にその記号を書きなさい。 🎧 Track 88

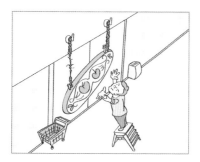

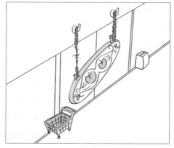

1. _____   2. _____   3. _____

will	been	were	had	would

Rika: Should I take the job in Okinawa or stay and look for one in Chiba?

Hideo: If I were you, I ₁( ) weigh both sides. Then go with the choice that you're most comfortable with.

Rika: Well, if the Okinawa company pays for a car or an apartment, I ₂( ) probably go that way.

Hideo: Is that your main consideration?

Rika: It's a big one. They aren't offering much of a salary. If the salary offer ₃( ) higher, I would definitely take the job.

Hideo: I was in a similar position a few years ago. I had a chance to work in Yokohama, but the benefits weren't very good. If they ₄( ) ₅( ) better, I would have made the move.

質問の答えとして最も適切なものを選びなさい。

1. ( ) What does Rika say about the job in Okinawa?
   A: The flight there will be free.   B: The company is large.
   C: The local area is beautiful.   D: The salary is not high.

2. ( ) Why didn't Hideo move to Yokohama?
   A: The salary offered by the company was low.
   B: The job did not come with good benefits.
   C: Finding a place to live in the city was too hard.
   D: He didn't want to live far away from Rika.

C **Writing** ( ) 内の語句を並べ替え、正しい文を作りなさい。

1. If (increase / the item / production / they will / sells well,).

_____

2. We (ourselves / knew how / the roof / if we / would repair).

_____

3. She (has one with / the store / a scarf if / may buy / flowers on it).

_____

A **Reading Passage**　次の英文を読み、(　　) 内の正しいほうの単語を選びなさい。

Bill is thinking about going to graduate school for an MBA. ₁If he goes full-time, he (will / would) have to quit his job. He could avoid that by studying part-time. ₂However, if he (chooses / chose) that option, it may take three years.

He has some money saved up. So if he enrolls in an intensive one-year program, it (would / will) not be a problem financially. Yet he has to consider his job. ₃If it (was / were) possible, the firm would let him take a year off. But they feel it's too long to leave his position empty.

Bill's mother thinks he should apply for a one-year MBA program. Years ago, she thought about going to grad school herself, but she didn't. If she (has / had) gotten her master's degree, it would have been a big help to her career.

NOTES　graduate school「大学院」　MBA「経営学修士 (Master of Business Administration)」
full-time「全日制で」　part-time「定時制で」　enroll「入学する」　intensive「集中的な」
financially「経済的に」　take a year off「1 年間休む」　apply for「…に申し込む」

B **Comprehension**　それぞれの文の内容が正しければ T(true) を、誤りであれば F(false) を○で囲みなさい。

1. If Bill goes to school part-time, his company will pay for it.　　T　F

2. The passage says Bill has money in the bank.　　T　F

3. Bill's company and his mother have different opinions.　　T　F

C Translation　前ページの英文の中で、下線が引かれている文を日本語に訳しなさい。

1. _____

2. _____

3. _____

Reference Material

---

if を使わない条件文　Other Types of Conditionals

1. My employer will pay for the trip **provided** I write a detailed report.

2. **As long as** there's room in the car, I'm fine with Dave riding with us.

3. You can stay with us for a few days **as long as** my wife doesn't mind.

4. Let's get some more bottles of water **in case** we need them later.

5. **In case** you change your mind, my offer for the painting stands.

6. **On the condition that** he phone his mother twice a day, the teenager was allowed to go on the trip.

7. **In the event of** an earthquake, stay away from the windows.

8. **In the event that** a flight is oversold, passengers are given refunds or vouchers for a future flight.

9. **Should** you need me while I'm away, here's my cell phone number.

10. Please contact me day or night **should** you have any questions.

仮定法では接続詞の if がよく使われるが、if の代わりに使って「もし…ならば」という意味を表すことのできる語句がいくつかある。

provided（仮に…とすれば）、as long as（…である限りは）、in case（もし…なら）、on the condition that（…という条件で）、in the event (of / that)（万一…の場合には）、should（もし…なら）

目的語となる　As Objects Track 89

He is trying to figure out **who made the sculpture**.

I don't know **how they fit so many toys on the shelves**.

I finally learned **where that mysterious tunnel goes**.

1. I know **what you mean**.
   あなたが言いたいことは、わかります。

2. We found out **where the shop is**.
   私たちは、その店がどこにあるのか見つけた。

3. I'm not sure **when Frank will arrive**.
   フランクがいつ到着するのか、わかりません。

> 主語と動詞を備えた1つの文が、「…ということ」という意味のひとかたまりの名詞の働きをするものを名詞節という。名詞節は目的語として使うことができる。名詞節を作るときは、関係代名詞 what、疑問詞、that や whether などの接続詞が使われ、節の中の語順は「主語＋述語」となる。

主語となる　As Subjects Track 90

How we're going to arrive on time is an excellent question.

That the stadium improved their food selection is welcome news.

When the water level will recede is hard to say.

1. **What my friend said** is true.
   私の友達が言ったことは本当です。

2. **How he earned his money** remains a mystery.
   彼がどうやってお金を稼いだのかは、謎のままだ。

3. **Where the event will take place** is an open question.
   そのイベントをどこで開催するのかは、議論の余地がある。

> 名詞節は、主語として使うこともできる。その場合、名詞節は常に単数として扱われる。

Do you know **what this jacket is made of**?

Can you tell me **where the light bulbs are**?

Are you sure **there are no more flights to Geneva today**?

1. Do you know **when the fireworks start**?
   その花火大会がいつ始まるのか知っていますか。

2. Would you happen to know **who he is**?
   もしかして彼が誰なのか、ご存じですか。

3. Have you heard **what the price will be**?
   価格がいくらになるのか、聞いていますか。

> 疑問詞で始まる名詞節は、疑問文の中で使って具体的な質問の内容を表すことができる。

Grammar Exercises

A （　）内の指示に従って、次の文を書き換えなさい。

[例]　He knows what the formula is.（疑問文に）

　　→ Does he know what the formula is?

1. It worries me that summers are becoming so hot.（名詞節を文頭に置いて）

   _____

2. We believe what Dan told us.（否定文に）

   _____

3. Do the police know who committed the crime?（平叙文に）

   _____

4. Why the road is still closed isn't clear.（名詞節をうしろに置いて）

   _____

5. Professor Ikeda will tell us what we should study for the test.（疑問文に）

   _____

B （　　）内の正しい語を選び、文を完成させなさい。

1. I'm not sure (where / why) the mall is. I'll look for the address online.

2. (How / What) we are supposed to raise one million yen in two weeks is a very good question.

3. Did she say (when / where) she's coming back? The coffee shop closes soon.

4. We're still trying to determine (what / why) the power went out.

5. Could you show me (how / where) the remote control works?

C 次の文の空欄に、適切な単語を入れて名詞節を作りなさい。

1. A: Can you tell me _____ the shift manager is?
   B: Sure. It's Mr. Nakamura. Do you need to talk to him?

2. A: That was an interesting meeting. Judith didn't say _____ we might open a new branch. Is it going to be in Singapore?
   B: Probably, but I'm not sure _____ the plan will go forward. It might not be until July.

3. A: _____ they made changes to the schedule so late bothers me.
   B: I know _____ you mean. The planning could be a lot better.

Skill Building

A **Listening**　3つの文(A, B, C)を聞き、それぞれの内容と一致しているイラストの下にその記号を書きなさい。　🎧 Track 92

1. _____　　　2. _____　　　3. _____

Speaking 次の会話文を読み、以下のリストから適切な単語を選んで空欄を埋めなさい。

why	who	how	that	where

Abe: You're a camera expert. Can you show me ₁(   ) this camera's video function works?

Ruth: Sure. First choose the image resolution...like so. You can also choose a mode, such as black and white. You can even shoot in slow motion.

Abe: Wow, that's a lot to remember. ₂(   ) they make cameras so complicated is a mystery.

Ruth: Camera makers think ₃(   ) people want a lot of functions.

Abe: That's true. I really should look for a tutorial. Do you know ₄(   ) I could find something like that?

Ruth: The Internet, for sure. I can show you one of the best websites. I'm not sure ₅(   ) runs it. My guess is he's a professional photographer.

質問の答えとして最も適切なものを選びなさい。

1. (   ) Which video function is not mentioned by Ruth?
   A: Image resolution   B: Sharing on social media
   C: Slow motion   D: Black and white mode

2. (   ) What does Ruth recommend?
   A: Buying a different camera
   B: Taking a university class
   C: Joining a photography club
   D: Visiting a good website

Writing 次の2つの文を、与えられている語句を使って1つの文にしなさい。

1. Madeline left her boyfriend. / That surprised us.

   It _____ that _____.

2. Can you tell me something? / I need to know where the toy section is.

   Can _____ where _____ ?

3. Nobody knows what the ad is trying to say. / It's unclear.

   What the _____ is _____.

A **Reading Passage** 次の英文を読み、(   )内の正しいほうの単語を選びなさい。

For most of us, going to the store and walking down the street are common actions. For celebrities, though, even simple things like these can be difficult. Some celebrities wear disguises when they go out. That way, people won't know (why / who) they are. ₁(That / What) they're constantly recognized is exciting at first. Over time, though, it becomes a burden.

Reporters called "paparazzi" follow celebrities around. Cameras in hand, they want to know (where / how) celebrities are at all times. ₂They even figure out (what / when) and where stars go on vacation. That's why many stars hire bodyguards. They don't feel safe without them. ₃Can you imagine (why / how) celebrities feel? They are sometimes described as living "in a bubble." Their every move is watched by the world.

NOTES celebrity「セレブ、有名人」 disguise「変装」 recognize「(人の素性が)わかる」 burden「重荷、精神的な負担」 paparazzi「有名人を追い回すカメラマン」 figure out「探り出す」 bubble「シャボン玉、密閉された空間」 move「行動」

B **Comprehension** それぞれの文の内容が正しければ T(true) を、誤りであれば F(false) を○で囲みなさい。

1. In daily life, celebrities wear disguises to appear more mysterious.　T　F

2. Stars hire paparazzi for protection.　T　F

3. The passage suggests celebrities have very little privacy.　T　F

1. _____

2. _____

3. _____

Reference Material

文の中で名詞節を作るもの　Chart of Noun Clause Types

		例
接続詞	目的語となる	I know **(that)** S + V ...
		She asked me **if / whether** S + V ...
	主語となる	**That** S + V is ...
		It doesn't matter **if** S + V ...
	補語となる	The fact is **(that)** S + V ...
		The question is **whether** S + V ...
	同格となる	They knew **(that)** S + V ...
		There is some doubt **whether / if** S + V ...
関係詞	目的語となる	I don't know **what** S + V ...
		He told us **how** S + V ...
	主語となる	**What** I say is ...
		Whoever comes is ...
	補語となる	This is **what** S + V ...
		The best time is **when** S + V ...
疑問詞	目的語となる	We found out **where** S + V ...
		I don't know **why** S + V ...
	補語となる	The question is **how** S + V ...

1. She asked me **if the product launch will be delayed**.

2. The fact is **everyone wants Violet to lead the department**.

3. There is some doubt **whether the dam can be repaired**.

4. **Whoever comes** is going to have a great time.

5. I don't know **why the train station lockers are so small**.

24 現在完了　Present Perfect

過去の経験や完了した行為・出来事を表す　Past Actions Track 94

I **have received** the samples.

The studio **hasn't finished** filming the movie.

Have you **given** the dog a bath this week?

1. I **have washed** all the dishes.
   食器をすべて洗い終えました。

2. He **hasn't heard** the joke.
   彼はそのジョークを聞いたことがなかった。

3. **Have** they **delivered** the new brochures yet?
   新しいパンフレットはまだ届いていないのですか。

> 「…し終わった」「…したことがある」と、現在から見て過去の行為や出来事について述べるときは、現在完了形を使う。現在完了は、have (has) のあとに動詞の過去分詞を置いて作る。否定文は have (has) のあとに not を加えて作り、疑問文は文頭に Have (Has) を置いて作る。

過去から現在までの継続を表す　Duration Track 95

She **has been** there more than 20 minutes.

The panda exhibit **hasn't been** open long.

How long **have** you **worked** as a bee keeper?

1. Mike **has lived** in Kokura since 1997.
   マイクは1997年からずっと小倉に住んでいる。

2. I **haven't seen** him for three years.
   私はこの3年間、彼と会っていない。

3. How long **have** you **been** here?
   ここには、どれくらいいるのですか。

> 「これまで…していた」と、過去のある時点から現在まで継続している行為や状態を表す場合にも、現在完了が使われる。その場合、since ... （…以来）や for ... （…の間）などの期間を示す語句が添えられることが多い。「これまでどれくらい？」と、期間を尋ねる場合は、疑問詞を使って How long have (has) ... ? のように尋ねる。

The school has **rarely** seen such a gifted athlete.

I'm afraid I haven't spoken to Hikari **recently**.

Have you **ever** played against that team?

1. The marketing director has **already** left the office.
   マーケティング部長は、もう会社を出ている。

2. She has **never** been to Brazil.
   彼女は、これまで一度もブラジルに行ったことがない。

3. Have you **ever** gone skydiving?
   あなたは今まで、スカイダイビングをしたことがありますか。

---

already（すでに）、never（一度も）、ever（これまでに）、just（たった今）、recently（最近）、often（しばしば）、seldom（めったに…ない）、since（…以来）、certainly（間違いなく）など、現在完了とともによく使われて、その意味を補足する副詞がいくつかある。

Grammar Exercises

(A) 次の文を、（　）内の動詞を使って現在完了の文にしなさい。

[例] She _____ _____ here since 9:30. (be)

　→ She <u>has</u> <u>been</u> here since 9:30.

1. I _____ not _____ the new baby videos yet. (upload)

2. Two of my friends _____ already _____ the exhibition. (see)

3. How long _____ you _____ as an executive assistant? (work)

4. John and Donovan _____ _____ in Japan since 2003. (live)

5. _____ he ever _____ a solo art show? (have)

6. No, we _____ never _____ Sweden. (visit)

7. He _____ _____ as a landscaper for 15 years. (work)

8. This _____ certainly _____ a memorable party! (be)

B （　）内の正しい語を選び、文を完成させなさい。

1. Most of the candidates (has / have) submitted their proposals.

2. Karen has (become / became) very good at her job.

3. We have (ever / never) gone scuba diving.

4. How many plays (you have / have you) acted in?

5. The deadline (already has / has already) passed.

C 次の文を読み、A と B のうち内容が正しいほうを選びなさい。

1. From 2016 to 2019, Hoshina was a student at the London School of Economics. As a student, he worked very hard. He wanted to visit Cambridge and York in England, but he didn't have the time. Now he is back in Japan.
   (A) Hoshina has never visited York.
   (B) Hoshina has been to Cambridge.

2. From 2001 to 2009, Laurie lived in New York. In 2009, she moved to Boston. She still lives in Boston.
   (A) Laurie has lived in New York since 2001.
   (B) Laurie has lived in Boston since 2009.

3. They started painting the office at 8:00 AM. At noon, they took a break for lunch. Then they continued their task. They are still painting the office.
   (A) They haven't finished painting the office.
   (B) They haven't had lunch yet.

Skill Building

A **Listening**　3つの文(A, B, C)を聞き、それぞれの内容と一致しているイラストの下にその記号を書きなさい。　🎧 Track 97

1. _____　　　2. _____　　　3. _____

B **Speaking** 次の会話文を読み、以下のリストから適切な単語を選んで空欄を埋めなさい。

have	has	been	had	how

Jessica: Hi, I'm Jessica. I'm new to the building – to the area, actually.

Alan: Nice to meet you. I'm Alan. Where are you from originally?

Jessica: Baltimore. Have you ever 1( ) there?

Alan: Once, around 15 years ago. I went there to visit Edgar Allen Poe's house. But I haven't 2( ) a chance to go back yet.

Jessica: The city 3( ) changed a lot since you visited. Anyway, this seems like a nice building. 4( ) long 5( ) you lived here?

Alan: About five years. I think you'll like it. Everyone's very friendly.

Jessica: That's good to know.

質問の答えとして最も適切なものを選びなさい。

1. ( ) What do we learn about Alan and Jessica's building?
   A: A famous person lives there.   B: It's in downtown Baltimore.
   C: The residents are friendly.   D: It was built 15 years ago.

2. ( ) What does Jessica say about Baltimore?
   A: It's different from the way it used to be.
   B: She lived there for five years.
   C: Most tourists enjoy visiting Poe's house.
   D: The city is a friendly place to live.

C **Writing** ( ) 内の語句を並べ替え、正しい文を作りなさい。

1. I (man / seen / before / that / have).

_____

2. How (wanted / have you / an actor / long / to be)?

_____

3. Donna (her / changed / has / e-mail address / never).

_____

Grammar Through Reading

A **Reading Passage**　次の英文を読み、（　）内の正しいほうの語(句)を選びなさい。

Cats is one of the most successful musicals of all time. The show, featuring dancers and singers in elaborate cat costumes, was created by Andrew Lloyd Webber. Most of the lyrics are based on songs and poems by T.S. Eliot. The show debuted in 1981 in London. ₁Since then, (there have / have there) been productions in over 30 countries. ₂Theater lovers in more than 300 cities (has / have) seen the musical.

Over the years, *Cats* has (winning / won) numerous awards, including the Tony for Best Musical. The show is one of many successful productions by Lloyd Webber. He has (creating / created) other classics, including *The Phantom of the Opera* and *Evita*. ₃Through his works, he has (ever / certainly) helped make musical theater more popular.

NOTES　feature「主演させる、…を呼び物にする」 elaborate「凝った、念入りに作った」
lyrics「歌詞」debut「初めて舞台に登場する」 production「上演、作品」 award「賞」
Tony「トニー賞」 classic「最高傑作」

B **Comprehension**　それぞれの文の内容が正しければ T(true) を、誤りであれば F(false) を○で囲みなさい。

1. *Cats* started running more than four decades ago.　　T　F

2. A "Tony" is a type of musical.　　T　F

3. Andrew Lloyd Webber wrote all the lyrics for *Cats*.　　T　F

C **Translation**　前ページの英文の中で、下線が引かれている文を日本語に訳しなさい。

1. _____

2. _____

3. _____

Reference Material

現在完了とともによく使われるその他の語句
Other Terms Used with the Present Perfect

now（たった今）、yet（まだ、もう）、lately（最近）、before（以前に）、once（かつて、一度）、sometimes（何度か）、... time(s)（…回）、up to ...（…に至るまで）、so far（これまでのところ）なども、現在完了とともによく使われる表現である。

1. The last runner has just **now** crossed the finish line.

2. The ballet hasn't started **yet**.

3. I haven't seen him around **lately**.

4. Have you eaten at this diner **before**?

5. Katriana has only beaten the badminton master **once**.

6. **Sometimes**, the younger team has won. But typically the more experienced team has been victorious.

7. How many **times** have you been to Malaysia?

8. On occasion, **up to** 30,000 migrating birds have been seen in the wetlands.

9. We have signed up eight volunteers **so far**.

過去の出来事の発生順　Sequencing Past Actions Track 98

We arrived at 8:30.
The party **had** already
started.

Shortly into the camping
trip, we realized we **hadn't
brought** enough food.

Is the scratch something
you **had seen** before
renting the car?

1. I went to the store to buy some milk. The kids **had drunk** it all.
   その店にはミルクを買いに行きました。子どもたちが全部飲んでしまったので。

2. It was cold in the gallery. I **hadn't anticipated** that.
   その美術館は寒かった。私はそれを予想していなかった。

3. Was becoming a chef something you **had** always **wanted** to do?
   シェフになったのは、あなたがずっとしたかったことですか。

> 過去完了は、過去のある時点を基準として、それ以前に起きた出来事を表わす。完了形を作る助動詞 have を had にし、その後に動詞の過去分詞を続けると「（過去のある時点までに）…し終えていた／ずっと…だった」という意味になる。

名詞句の中の過去完了　With Noun Clauses Track 99

We suspected the
equipment **had been
tampered with**.

After returning from vacation,
Jeff noticed the office **had
been rearranged**.

Were you aware the
host **had expanded**
the guest list?

1. I thought that you **had finished** the report.
   あなたはもう報告書を書き終えていたのかと思っていました。

2. Did you know the meeting **had been postponed**?
   会議が延期されていたことを知っていましたか。

3. Kevin showed me how the earthquake **had damaged** the wall.
   ケビンは、地震がその壁にどれくらい被害を及ぼしたのか私に見せてくれた。

> 主節の動詞が過去形で目的語に名詞節をとる場合、その名詞節内で示されている出来事が主節の動詞以前に起きたことをはっきり示したいときに過去完了形が使われる。

Track 100

By the time the food came, we **had been waiting** 45 minutes.

I **hadn't been living** in the area long, so the earthquake was surprising.

Was the supply shortage a problem you **had been anticipating**?

1. Before Debra left Chicago, she **had been living** there for 16 years.
   デブラはシカゴを離れるまで、そこに 16 年間住んでいた。

2. Haruto packed very little. He **hadn't been expecting** to extend the trip.
   ハルトは荷物をわずかしか詰めなかった。旅行を延長することになると予想していなかったからだ。

3. Was the move something the company **had been planning** a long time?
   その措置は、会社が長い間計画していたものだったのだろうか。

> 「…したときまでずっと…していた」のように、過去のある時点まで、何らかの動作がその前から続いていたことを表わす場合に過去完了進行形が使われる。その文は「had ＋ been ＋現在分詞」の形をとる。

Grammar Exercises

A （　　）内の動詞を過去完了の形にして、文を完成させなさい。

[例] We arrived at the theater at 8:15. The play _____ already _____. (start)
   → We arrived at the theater at 8:15. The play <u>had</u> already <u>started</u>.

1. Originally, I _____ _____ to take a train to Prague. (plan)
   I changed my mind and took a plane instead.

2. There weren't enough chairs because the event organizers _____
   only _____ 50 people to attend. (expect)

3. Did you say you _____ _____ to finish by 5:00? (hope)

4. Before yesterday's video chat, they _____ not _____ for
   12 years. (speak)

5. Meeting the author was the highlight of my month. I _____
   _____ to meet her since I was a child. (want)

B 次の文のあとに続く表現の記号を、空欄に書き入れなさい。

1. Before the nail salon closed, I had _____
2. Greece was perfect. We had been _____
3. Gwen had heard the garden _____
4. Do you know why they had been _____

(A) looking forward to traveling there for a long time.

(B) considering changing the date?

(C) been working there for 11 years.

(D) was beautiful. Seeing it in person was unforgettable.

C それぞれの質問に対し、（　　）内の語句を使った過去完了の文で答えなさい。

1. In the middle of the outdoor festival, it started to rain. We got wet since we had expected the weather to be nice all day.
   (A) Before the festival, they knew it was going to rain.
   (B) They probably didn't bring umbrellas or raincoats to the festival.

2. Michelle had never dreamed of becoming a world-famous pop star. Her success surprised her as much as anyone else.
   (A) Michelle had not planned to become so well known.
   (B) Since she was a child, Michelle's goal was to become famous.

3. Anthony, the restaurant's owner, had been doing all the food deliveries himself. Eventually, he hired a driver to handle deliveries.
   (A) Anthony was hired by the restaurant to deliver food.
   (B) After hiring a driver, Anthony didn't need to deliver food himself.

Skill Building

A **Listening** 3つの文（A, B, C）を聞き、それぞれの内容と一致しているイラストの下にその記号を書きなさい。 🎧 Track 101

1. _____   2. _____   3. _____

B **Speaking** 次の会話文を読み、以下のリストから適切な単語を選んで空欄を埋めなさい。

| remember | had | doing | planting | hoping |

Daisy: What are you ₁(　　　　　)?

Jake: Two rows of apple trees. I ₂(　　　　　) planned to do it last year, but Mark was away visiting relatives. We were short on help.

Daisy: I ₃(　　　　　). You had your hands full.

Jake: Yeah. We had originally been ₄(　　　　　) to make this a large apple orchard. The strawberries grew so well that we focused on those.

Daisy: Maybe you can do both now. I love apple picking in the fall.

Jake: Hopefully in a few years we can start ₅(　　　　　) that here.

質問の答えとして最も適切なものを選びなさい。

1. (　　) Where does Jake probably work?
　　A: On a farm　　　　　　B: At a travel agency
　　C: At a supermarket　　　D: At Daisy's company

2. (　　) What does Jake say about strawberries?
　　A: He had always planned to make them the main crop.
　　B: Strawberries grow very well on his land.
　　C: Daisy can pick strawberries on the farm anytime she likes.
　　D: Apples are easier to grow than strawberries.

C **Writing** それぞれの質問に対し、(　　　) 内の語句を使った過去完了の文で答えなさい。

[例] Before moving, how long had they lived in the house? (18 years)
　　→ <u>They had lived in the house 18 years.</u>

1. How long had you been thinking about opening the store? (two years)

　　I _____

2. Why didn't you guys wear coats last night? (expected, weather, to be warm)

　　We _____

3. During the trip, you knew everything about Italy. How did you learn so much about the country? (read a few books, talked to some Italian students)

　　I had _____

Grammar Through Reading

 Reading Passage　次の英文を読み、(　　)内の正しいほうの単語を選びなさい。

After graduating from art school, Cheryl knew exactly what she wanted to do. ₁From a young age, she had (dreamed / dreaming) of becoming a children's book illustrator. There was something magical about connecting beautiful art with exciting stories.

To learn more about the field, Cheryl got a job at a children's book publisher. There she met Max, the chief designer. Max became a mentor, helping Cheryl refine her craft. ₂She (was / had) always had trouble drawing hands. Max shared a technique which helped her smooth out the problem.

After several years, Cheryl was ready to branch out on her own. She left the publisher and set up a home studio. Her goal was to create a series of books using a cat or other animal as the main character. ₃She had been (influenced / influencer) by authors who created their own interesting characters. Would Cheryl be as successful as Beatrix Potter (*Peter Rabbit*) or Norman Bridwell (*Clifford the Big Red Dog*)? She was going to give it her best and find out!

NOTES　graduate「卒業する」 exactly「正確に」 field「(学問・芸術などの) 分野」 mentor「指導者」
refine「(技術などに) 磨きをかける」 have trouble -ing「…するのに苦労する」 smooth out「(問題を)
取り除く」branch out「(新しいことに) 手を広げる」 Peter Rabbit「児童文学作品『ピーターラビット
のお話』」Clifford the Big Red Dog「児童文学作品『おおきいあかいクリフォード』」
give it one's best「全力を尽くす」

 Comprehension　それぞれの文の内容が正しければ T(true) を、誤りであれば
F(false) を○で囲みなさい。

1. Before attending art school, Cheryl wanted to be a teacher.　　　T　F

2. Max helped Cheryl become a better illustrator.　　　T　F

3. In Cheryl's books, the main character might be a young girl.　　　T　F

C **Translation** 前ページの英文の中で、下線が引かれている文を日本語に訳しなさい。

1. _____

2. _____

3. _____

--- **Reference Material** ---

過去完了の３つの用法 Three Basic Uses of the Past Perfect

1. By the time we arrived at the ballroom, the dance contest **had** already **started**.（完了）

2. She **had never ridden** a horse before she visited the farm.（経験）

3. Since I **hadn't had** enough sleep, I was feeling a bit light-headed.（継続）

現在完了と同様に、過去完了にも「すでに〜して［し終えて］いた」という完了、それより前に〜したことがあった［なかった］（経験）、「それ以前からずっと〜だった」（継続）の意味を表す用法がある。

過去完了とその他の時制の組み合わせ Combination of Past Perfect and Other Tenses

1. Yesterday I found the keys **I'd lost** in the park.（過去＋過去完了）

2. I wish I **had never bought** that car.（仮定法）

3. If you **had gone** to the party, you could have met my brother.（仮定法）

4. That was the funniest thing I've [**I'd**] ever **heard**.（過去＋現在［過去］完了）

5. Tom said he was born [×**had been born**] in Fukuoka, Japan.（過去＋過去）

過去完了は過去時制とともに用いられることが多いが、その他の時制と組み合わせた表現もある。２と３は仮定法過去の例。４は、過去のある時点までのことであれば過去完了を、現在にも当てはまることなら現在完了を使う。５のように、時間の前後が明白な場合は、文の構造が簡単な過去形を使う。

26 未来完了　Future Perfect

  Track 102

By dinner time, he **will have finished** painting the fence.

At 4:00 PM, the store **will not have closed** for the day.

Will they **have completed** the bridge's construction before July 15?

1. In 20 minutes, the movie **will have started**.
   20分後には、その映画が始まっているでしょう。

2. The judges **will not have decided** on a winner by noon.
   審査員たちは、正午までに優勝者を決めることはないでしょう。

3. Come September, we **will have known** each other for 13 years.
   9月になると、私たちは知り合って13年経つことになります。

> 「（…までには）…していることだろう」のように、未来のある時点までに何らかの動作が始まっていたり、完了していたり、経験していたり、状態が継続したりしている場合に未来完了が使われる。その文は「will + have +過去分詞」の形をとる。

  Track 103

The office **will have been cleaned** before the CEO arrives.

As soon as I collect one more signature, I **will have filled up** the whole sheet.

When Bob speaks with Lisa, **will** he **have met** with everyone in the department?

1. When the team wins, they **will have captured** six championships.
   そのチームが勝つと、6つの優勝タイトルを獲得していることになる。

2. Before a decision is made, every option **will have been considered**.
   決定が下される前に、すべての選択肢が検討されているだろう。

3. **Will** the news **have been announced** by the time the market opens?
   市場が開くまでに、そのニュースは公表されているだろうか。

> 主節の文で未来完了が使われていても、時や条件を表す副詞節や形容詞節の中では、未来の出来事であっても will を使わずに現在形を用いる。例えば、上の文では、それぞれ will win や will be made、will open などとしないこと。

Track 104

At 3:45, he **will have been waiting** there exactly two hours.

By winter, this train line **will have been operating** for 25 years.

When the clock strikes 10:00, the guard **will have been standing** there three hours.

1. Come April, we **will have been living** in this town for 11 years.
   4月になると、私たちはこの町に11年間住み続けていることになる。

2. When the fiscal year starts, Jacques **will have been working** as a financial advisor for seven years.
   会計年度が始まると、ジャックは7年間、投資顧問として働いていることになる。

3. I love this bank. By next year, I **will have been banking** here for 30 years.
   私はこの銀行がとても気に入っている。来年までに、私はここで30年間取引していることになる。

> 未来のある時点においても現在の出来事が引き続き進行中であることを表わす場合に、未来完了進行形が使われる。その文は「will have been ＋現在分詞」の形をとる。

Grammar Exercises

A （　　）内の動詞を未来完了形にして、それぞれの文を完成させなさい。

[例] By Friday, the schedule will ＿＿＿＿＿＿ been ＿＿＿＿＿＿. (determine)

　　 → By Friday, the schedule will <u>have</u> been <u>determined</u>.

1. As soon as someone buys this muffin, I will ＿＿＿＿＿＿ ＿＿＿＿＿＿ out of my baked goods. (sell)

2. Experts fear the company will not ＿＿＿＿＿＿ ＿＿＿＿＿＿ its distribution problems by the start of the third quarter. (solve)

3. Will they ＿＿＿＿＿＿ ＿＿＿＿＿＿ the roadwork by the time the monsoon season begins? (complete)

4. The successor to the throne will ＿＿＿＿＿＿ been ＿＿＿＿＿＿ before the upcoming national celebration. (decide)

5. In 2045, the landmark will ＿＿＿＿＿＿ been ＿＿＿＿＿＿ here for 200 years. (stand［未来完了進行形で］)

B （　　）内の指示に従って各文を書き換えなさい。

[例] She will have left by 3:30.（否定文に変更）

→ <u>She will not have left by 3:30.</u>

1. The limited-edition shoes will not have sold out.（肯定文に変更）

_____

2. Will the rule have been changed before the tournament starts?（平叙文に変更）

_____

3. They will have announced the ceremony's date by Sunday.（疑問文に変更）

_____

C 次の文を読み、その内容を正しく表しているものを A と B のどちらかから選びなさい。

1. Roy needs to get here soon. In 20 minutes, all of the food will have been eaten.
   (A) If Roy arrives in 30 minutes, he won't have anything to eat.
   (B) There is plenty of food left, so there's no need for Roy to rush.

2. By next year, they will have been working on the project for eight years.
   (A) They have been working on the project for more than five years.
   (B) It's going to take another eight years to finish the project.

3. The gala is on the 25th. By the 23rd, the palace will have been decorated.
   (A) It will not be possible to decorate the palace before the date of the gala.
   (B) The palace will be decorated before the gala takes place.

Skill Building

A **Listening** 3つの文(A, B, C)を聞き、それぞれの内容と一致しているイラストの下にその記号を書きなさい。 🎧 Track 105

1. _____   2. _____   3. _____

B **Speaking** 次の会話文を読み、以下のリストから適切な単語を選んで空欄を埋めなさい。

been	summer	going	opened	must

Phil: I love that you're opening a restaurant. Is everything 1( ) well?

Isabelle: Most things are, but the license application is slow. I'm worried that by the time we get it, other restaurants will have 2( ) nearby.

Phil: Hmm...Could more restaurants possibly draw more people to the area?

Isabelle: They could. That's a good point. I guess I'm just getting impatient. By next week, we will have 3( ) waiting three months.

Phil: I'm sorry. That 4( ) be frustrating.

Isabelle: A little. We'd love to be open by 5( ). Our outdoor seating area will be perfect for the warmer months.

質問の答えとして最も適切なものを選びなさい。

1. ( ) What's taking a long time?
  A: Building the outdoor area B: Getting a restaurant license
  C: Attracting new customers D: Finding an experienced chef

2. ( ) What is Isabelle worried about?
  A: Her outdoor seating area may not be large enough.
  B: The cost of the license may be high.
  C: Phil might not be able to help her.
  D: It's possible that more restaurants will open in the area.

C **Writing** ( ) 内の語句を並べ替え、正しい文を作りなさい。

1. The (gone down / sun / 7:30 / will have / by).

_____

2. Will the (before / to Sapporo / snow / we drive / have melted)?

_____

3. In May (been married / 25 years / will have / for / we).

_____

Grammar Through Reading

Ⓐ Reading Passage　次の英文を読み、(　　) 内の正しいほうの単語を選びなさい。

Tower Bridge, which crosses the Thames River, is one of London's most famous landmarks. In the late 19th century, hundreds of workers used more than 10,000 tons of steel to build the beautiful yet practical structure. After eight years of construction, the bridge opened in 1894. ₁By 2044, it will (have been / having been) in service for 150 years.

The sides of the bridge lift to allow large boats to pass through. Every day, the bridge is also crossed by more than 40,000 people. It is used by locals and out-of-town visitors like Claude and Mindy Walker. ₂After their trip to London, the couple will have (visited / visiting) 25 world capitals. Several years ago, they started live streaming parts of their journeys. ₃When they (stream / streaming) their walk across Tower Bridge, they will have shared 15 special experiences with the world.

NOTES　Tower Bridge「タワーブリッジ（ロンドンにあるテムズ川にかかる可動橋)」 landmark「歴史的建造物」 practical「有用な」 in service「稼働して」 capital「（国の）首都」 live stream「ネット上で動画を生中継する」 share ... with ...「…を…に伝える」

Ⓑ Comprehension　それぞれの文の内容が正しければ T(true) を、誤りであれば F(false) を○で囲みなさい。

1. It took eight years to build Tower Bridge. 　　　　　　　　T　F

2. Large boats on the Thames River can pass through the bridge. 　T　F

3. Claude and Mindy have live streamed more than 25 times. 　　T　F

C **Translation** 前ページの英文の中で、下線が引かれている文を日本語に訳しなさい。

1. _____

2. _____

3. _____

―――――――――― **Reference Material** ――――――――――

未来完了を単純未来で言い換える Using the Simple Future to Express the Future Perfect

1. The experiment **will have been completed** by the end of the week.
   → The experiment **will be completed** by the end of the week.
2. The stage **will have been set up** by the time you get back.
   → The stage **will be set up** by the time you get back.

未来完了は、単純未来（will ＋動詞の原形）で置き換えることができる場合がある。

未来完了進行形と動詞の種類 The Future Perfect and Certain Verb Types

1. John will be tired when he eats lunch because he **will have already been working** for five hours.
2. Come next year, Alice **will have belonged** (×have been belonging) to the choral group for six years.

未来完了進行形は原則として動作動詞について使われ、状態動詞（believe, belong to, know, live, remain など）で使われることはない。ただし、同じ動詞でも動作動詞と状態動詞の両方の用法を持つものがあることに注意。

時を表わす副詞句の中 Adverb Clauses Starting with a Time Indicator

1. I will lend you the comic book once I (×will) **have finished** reading it.
2. As soon as we (×will) **have decided**, we will let you know.
3. After the mechanic **has fixed** (×will have fixed) the air conditioner, the car will be more comfortable.

意味的には未来完了であっても、時を表わす接続詞が導く節の中では現在（完了）形が使われる。

27 間接・直接話法 Indirect and Direct Speech

Francine **said** she loved the striped sweater.

Everyone **said** they wanted to stay at the beach longer.

Lindsey **told** me she planned to move to a bigger place.

1. My aunt **said** that she wanted to retire and travel around the world.
   私の叔母は、退職して世界中を旅行したいと言っていた。

2. The tour guide **told** us it was the oldest building in the city.
   そのツアーガイドは、それが市内で最も古い建物だと教えてくれた。

3. The taxi driver **asked** us where we wanted to go.
   タクシー運転手は、私たちにどこに行きたいのか尋ねた。

> 間接話法とは、人が発言した内容を、それを伝える者の立場から間接的に表現する方法。その内容は、say、tell、ask などの伝達動詞のあとで that（しばしば省略可）、if、whether などの節の中で示される。基本的に、伝達動詞が過去であれば、その後の節の中の動詞も過去となる（時制の一致）。

Manny **said** he eats a large, green salad every day.

The artist **told** the reporter he's working on a new series of paintings.

My classmates **answered** they would love to form a study group.

1. The electrician **said** he will be here at 3:30.
   その電気工は、3時30分にここに来ると言った（がまだ来ていない）。

2. Our neighbors **asked** if we could turn the music down.
   近所の人が、私たちに音楽の音量を下げてもらえないかと頼んできた。

3. The demonstrators **insist** they are marching to support animal rights.
   デモ参加者たちは、動物の権利を支援するために行進するつもりだと言い張っている。

> 間接話法は、さまざまな時制と組み合わせて使われる。1. で would が使われていれば、「過去にそうするつもりだった」ことを表すが、will が使われると、「まだそうするつもり＝動作を完了していない」ことを表わす。3. は現在形と未来を表わす現在進行形の組み合わせ。一般に、伝達動詞が過去形であっても、話された内容が現在も事実であれば、時制を変える必要はない。

Track 108

Kip's mom **said**, "Watch your brother while you're at the park."

The lifeguard **shouted**, "Everybody get out of the water!"

The little boy **asked**, "What ice cream flavors do you have?"

1. The captain **announced**, "On the left, you can see the Grand Canyon."
   機長は、「左側にはグランドキャニオンが見えます」と知らせてくれた。

2. I asked about sales. The cashier **replied**, "We run sales twice a year."
   私はバーゲンセールについて尋ねた。レジ係は「年に2回バーゲンセールをしています」と答えた。

3. "We'd better leave," Jack **said**, "or we'll miss the train."
   ジャックは、「出発したほうがいいですよ。さもないと電車に乗り遅れます」と言った。

> 直接話法とは、発言した人の言葉をそのまま引用する形で表したもので、その部分を引用符（" "）で囲む。引用部分は伝達動詞のうしろ、前、その両方のいずれの位置にも置くことができる。

Grammar Exercises

A （　）内の正しい語を選び、文を完成させなさい。

1. After the flight, Dad (said / told) he felt tired.

2. Lana (told / said) she will get the car dent repaired soon.

3. "Ms. Wilson," the interviewer (reported / asked), "what's the main reason you want to work here?"

4. I asked about the store's holiday hours. The salesperson (told / said) me they are open on holidays until 6:00 PM.

5. The agent (asked / told), "How large of an apartment do you need?"

6. I (asked / shouted) how much the cheese cost. The grocer said it depends on the type and weight of the cheese.

7. After reading the question aloud, the speaker (responded / told), "Our theory suggests there may be life on other planets."

B 次の文のあとに続く表現の記号を、空欄に書き入れなさい。

1. The painter said he will _____   (A) the office will be closed all week.

2. When I called, a recording said _____   (B) try and pay attention."

3. Ms. Endo said, "We'll reply _____   (C) you deliver the sofa today?"

4. "Tim," the teacher said, "please _____   (D) to your request by Friday."

5. The customer asked, "Can _____   (E) finish the job tomorrow.

C (　　) 内の指示に従って、それぞれの文を書き換えなさい。

[例] Lydia said she will attend the wedding. （直接話法に）

→ Lydia said, "I will attend the wedding."

1. Bill said, "I will meet everyone at the theater." （間接話法に）

_____

2. Kenji told us his goal is to become the CEO of a big company. （直接話法に）

_____

3. My colleague asked me when the meeting will start. （直接話法に）

_____

4. The man said, "The hotel is fully booked." （間接話法に）

_____

Skill Building

A **Listening**　3つの文(A, B, C)を聞き、それぞれの内容と一致しているイラストの
下にその記号を書きなさい。　🎧 Track 109

1. _____　　　　　2. _____　　　　　3. _____

B **Speaking** 次の会話文を読み、以下のリストから適切な単語を選んで空欄を埋めなさい。

need	going	feels	said	told

Anne: Is Maddy coming on the camping trip?

Kurt: She ₁(　　　　　) me she really wants to go. But her father will be away on business that weekend.

Anne: Is Maddy ₂(　　　　　) with him?

Kurt: No, but she said she may ₃(　　　　　) to watch her little brother.

Anne: Oh, that's right. Her mom works on Saturdays.

Kurt: Yeah. I remember Maddy's exact words. She ₄(　　　　　), "It isn't fair that I have to give up my trip to watch Kyle."

Anne: I know how she ₅(　　　　　). Being an older sister can be tough.

質問の答えとして最も適切なものを選びなさい。

1. (　) Who is Kyle?
    A: Kurt's friend　　　　　B: Anne's father
    C: Maddy's brother　　　　D: The trip leader

2. (　) Which of these statements is probably true?
    A: If Maddy doesn't go on the trip, it will be cancelled.
    B: Maddy's father works every weekend.
    C: Anne doesn't have any brothers or sisters.
    D: Saturday will be one of the days of the camping trip.

C **Writing** 次の2つの文を、与えられている語句を使って1つの文にしなさい。

1. Sachi told me something. / She wants to buy an electric car.

   Sachi _____ she _____.

2. The reporter asked a question. / She wanted to know what the budget will be.

   _____ asked, " _____ be?"

3. The dock worker shouted. / He told people to watch out for the high waves.

   _____ shouted, " _____ !"

Grammar Through Reading

A Reading Passage 次の英文を読み、(　　)内の正しいほうの単語を選びなさい。

Rising energy costs are an important topic in the town of Riverview. Compared to last year, the average electricity bill is up 22%. Last week, the city council held a town meeting to discuss the issue. ₁The chairperson (said / asked), "Let's work together to solve the problem." Then she asked people with questions or comments to line up behind the microphone.

Most people had similar concerns. They were worried about the high energy costs. ₂One man (asked / told), "Can you stop electricity prices from going up again?" The council said they couldn't make any promises. But they would make an emergency request to the utility company.

Other possible solutions were discussed. For example, Mary Santos, a blueberry farmer, asked the councilmembers about alternative energy. ₃She (said / told) them she wanted to install solar panels. However, the price was high. Could the government back interest-free loans? That idea interested the council, and they said they would seriously consider it.

NOTES city council「市議会」 chairperson「議長」 line up「(一列に) 並ぶ」 concern「心配、懸念」 emergency「緊急の」 utility company「(電気・水道・ガスなどの) 公共企業」 councilmember「議員」 alternative「代替の」 back「支援する」 interest-free「無利子の」

B Comprehension それぞれの文の内容が正しければ T(true) を、誤りであれば F(false) を○で囲みなさい。

1. Since last year, electricity costs have risen more than 20%.   T   F

2. The city council promised to lower energy costs.   T   F

3. Mary wants a loan to make her farm larger.   T   F

C **Translation**　前ページの英文の中で、下線が引かれている文を日本語に訳しなさい。

1. _____

2. _____

3. _____

——— Reference Material ———

間接話法＋過去完了形　Indirect Speech + Past Perfect Tense

1. The police **said** they **had discovered** important evidence in the apartment.

2. Our new mayor **announced** she **had created** a science advisory department.

3. The prominent researcher **admitted** he **had not reviewed** the latest data.

4. The electrician **insisted** he **had double-checked** the wiring.

過去のある時点よりも前の出来事を示す。

間接話法＋助動詞　Indirect Speech + Modals

1. The teacher **said** I **must** keep my phone off during class.

2. Mr. Cooper **asked** if we **might** like to see the racetrack during our visit.

3. My sister **said** we **could** stay for dinner.

4. When I asked her, the interviewee **replied** she **would** be happy to meet again.

過去形がない助動詞はそのままの形で使う。must の代わりに had to を使うことも可。

間接話法＋現在形　Indirect Speech + Present Tense

1. Jessica **said** her grandfather **takes** a walk every morning.

2. Goro **told** me he **loves** coming to this gallery.

3. Mike's parents **insisted** they **want** to help pay for the wedding.

4. My best friend **said** she **plans** to travel to Venezuela this summer.

現時点でも成り立つ事実は現在形を使う。

因果関係を表わす　Causation

 Track 110

Business was booming at the bakery. **Therefore**, it hired several more people.

It has been a cold and dry winter. **Because of that**, my skin is dry.

There weren't enough chairs. **For that reason**, some people had to stand.

1. Demand for new homes rose. **Consequently**, home prices went up.
   新築住宅の需要が高まった。その結果として、住宅価格が上昇した。

2. Javier started exercising daily. **As a result**, he lost a good deal of weight.
   ハビエルは毎日運動をすることにした。その結果、彼はかなり体重を減らした。

3. A tree fell and smashed our gate into pieces, **hence** the pile of wood over there.
   木が倒れてきて、門をばらばらに壊したので、あちらに木片の山ができている。

前の文を受けて、「その結果…」という原因と結果の関係を表わす副詞（句）がいくつかある。因果関係を表わす副詞には、therefore「それゆえに」、accordingly「したがって」、so「そういうわけで」、then「それで」などもある。

対比を表わす　Contrast

 Track 111

This hardware store has great deals. **In contrast**, other places are more expensive.

Not everyone is here yet. **Regardless**, we need to start the meeting.

The road is rough. **However**, our truck can handle it.

1. Most of us want to go bowling. **However**, Tom wants to see a movie.
   私たちのほとんどは、ボウリングをしに行きたい。でも、トムは映画を見たがっている。

2. It's just a little cloudy. **Then again**, the weather report called for rain later.
   少し曇っているだけだ。その一方、天気予報は後で雨が降ると報じている。

3. I love dark chocolate. **On the other hand**, my sister is a fan of milk chocolate.
   私はダークチョコレートが大好きです。一方、姉はミルクチョコレートが好みです。

「Aは…。その一方でBは…」のように2つの文を対比する副詞（句）がいくつかある。上の例以外に、by [in] contrast「それとは対照的に」、on the contrary「一方」、meanwhile「その一方で」、unlike「…とは違って」などがある。

情報を追加する　Addition　Track 112

Our cats love to be petted. **Likewise**, our dog asks everyone for attention.

I need two buckets of paint. **Additionally**, I'd like a paint roller, please.

The repair work will be difficult, **not to mention** time consuming.

1. We will remodel the showroom. **Furthermore**, we'll put in new lighting.
   私たちはショールームを改装する予定です。さらに、新しい照明を設置します。

2. There will be a full orchestra. **In addition**, a local choir will perform.
   フル・オーケストラが出演します。それに加えて、地元の合唱団が歌います。

3. Belize is famous for its wildlife. **Moreover**, the beaches are world-class.
   ベリーズは野生動物で有名です。さらに、そこのビーチは世界有数です。

> すでに述べたことに情報を追加するときに使う表現がいくつかある。also、likewise、plus、(then) again、on top of this/that、besides、furthermore などもよく使われる。

Grammar Exercises

A （　）内の正しい語（句）を選び、文を完成させなさい。

1. There was a hole in the roof. (Because / Because of that), water came in when it rained.

2. The price of the drill is a little over our budget. (Had / Having) said that, it would last a long time.

3. The parade will feature a marching band. (Additionally / Addition in), there will be giant balloons.

4. Bus fares went up. (As a result / Resulting), bus ridership decreased.

5. Those curtains are heavy and dark. (Contrasting / In contrast), these are light and bright.

6. You'll need a flashlight. (Further / Furthermore), an umbrella and a raincoat might be helpful.

B 次の文のあとに続く表現の記号を、空欄に書き入れなさい。

1. It was her first-ever soccer match. _____

2. We ran out of paper. Because of _____

3. Manuel will be promoted. _____

4. There was an accident, hence the _____

5. I was in favor of the merger. _____

(A) Morever, he will receive a pay raise and a company car.

(B) Nevertheless, she scored a goal.

(C) However, Jack was against it.

(D) that, I couldn't print the document.

(E) big traffic jam on the highway.

C 次の文を読み、その内容を正しく表しているものを A と B のどちらかから選びなさい。

1. The power went out during the storm. Consequently, the house was completely dark last night.
   (A) The house's lights went out before the storm.
   (B) The storm caused the lights to go out.

2. I understand everyone is tired. Regardless, we need to finish today.
   (A) They must finish today even though everyone is tired.
   (B) Because everyone is tired, they will finish another day.

3. During the hike, the path will be steep, not to mention narrow.
   (A) Although the path will be steep, it will not be narrow.
   (B) The path will be both steep and narrow.

Skill Building

A **Listening** 3つの文(A, B, C)を聞き、それぞれの内容と一致しているイラストの下にその記号を書きなさい。 🎧 Track 113

1. _____   2. _____   3. _____

because of	however	everything	likewise	when

Collin:　The art show is just a few days away. Is ₁(　　　　　) ready?

Renee:　Almost. We're still waiting for a few pieces. I've sent the artists reminders. ₂(　　　　　), three haven't delivered their work yet.

Collin:　It must be hard ₃(　　　　　) so many people are involved.

Renee:　It is, but the work is fantastic. ₄(　　　　　), the gallery looks amazing.

Collin:　That's awesome. Are you expecting a lot of visitors?

Renee:　We are. Only 35 people can fit inside the gallery. ₅(　　　　　) that, everyone will need to reserve a time and day to visit.

質問の答えとして最も適切なものを選びなさい。

1. (　　) What is Renee waiting to receive?
　　A: An invitation to the show　　B: Payment for her work
　　C: A reminder message　　D: Some pieces of art

2. (　　) Why will art lovers need to reserve a time to see the show?
　　A: There are some security concerns.
　　B: The gallery likes collecting visitors' personal information.
　　C: There is limited space in the gallery.
　　D: The works of art will only be displayed two hours a day.

C Writing　(　　) 内の語句を並べ替え、正しい文を作りなさい。

1. The (will / expensive / be / project). Furthermore, (six / will take / it / months).

　　_____

2. Our (is / spring break / short). In contrast, (is / our / long / summer vacation).

　　_____

3. The (being / is / repaired / tunnel). Because (it / of that, / closed / is).

　　_____

(A) Reading Passage 次の英文を読み、( )内の正しいほうの単語を選びなさい。

The Summer and Winter Olympics have been major global sporting events for over 100 years. More than 50 cities have held the honor of being called an Olympic city. There are clear advantages to hosting the games. ₁(Then again / Because of that), there are also major costs and risks.

The Olympics are a chance to showcase one's country to the world, bring positive media attention, and grow tourism. The UK, for instance, saw a tourism increase of 12% a full year after London's 2012 Summer Olympics. ₂(In addition / Regardless), the Olympics are a chance to build new roads, train lines, and so on.

However, hosting the games can have drawbacks. Some cities, like Los Angeles in 1984, turn a profit. Most, though, go over their budgets by billions of dollars and lose money. Also, expensive new stadiums often go unused after the Olympic torch is put out. ₃(Consequently / Not to mention), the games' organizers face a challenge. They need to maintain the Olympics' positive points while finding solutions to host cities' problems.

NOTES honor「名誉」 advantage「利点、メリット」 host「(イベントなどを) 主催する」
showcase「紹介する」 drawback「短所、不都合」 go over「…を超える」
put out「(火などを) 消す」

(B) Comprehension それぞれの文の内容が正しければ T(true) を、誤りであれば
F(false) を○で囲みなさい。

1. London only saw a tourism increase in 2012.　　　　　　　T　F

2. Many cities lose money by hosting the Olympics.　　　　　T　F

3. After the Olympics, cities always find ways to use stadiums.　T　F

1. _____

2. _____

3. _____

--- **Reference Material** ---

そのほかの重要なつなぎ言葉　Other Transitional Words and Phrases

1) 結論・要約 (concluding・summarizing)

つまり、要するに、結局　in short / in sum / in brief / in conclusion / in summary /
to summarize / in other words / basically / in a nutshell / in a word /
in fact / after all / in the end / eventually / finally / lastly /
at the end of the day / simply put

2) 明確化 (clarifying)

より正確に言えば　precisely speaking / more precisely / namely / or rather / to clarify

3) 言い換え (paraphrasing)

言い換えれば　that is (to say) / or / in other words / I mean / this means /
stated differently / to paraphrase

4) 総括 (generalizing)

概して　in general / generally speaking / overall / all in all / on the whole /
altogether / by and large

5) 具体例の提示 (exemplifying)

具体的に言うと　concretely (speaking) / specifically / for example [instance] /
to give an example / case in point

6) 強調 (emphasizing)

何よりも　above all (things) / most of all / first and foremost / best of all

過去の可能性を表わす　Possibility

 Track 114

The customer **may have decided** to buy a computer elsewhere.

Someone **could have placed** the bucket here in case the roof leaks.

Might the ring **have been turned in** to the lost and found counter?

1. The postal carrier **might have delivered** the package to a neighbor.
   もしかすると、郵便配達員は、その荷物を隣の家に配達したのかもしれない。

2. Erica **may not have told** you all the details about what happened.
   エリカは、起きたことの一部始終をあなたに話していなかったのかもしれない。

3. **Could** a wild animal **have caused** the damage?
   もしかして、野生動物がその被害をもたらした可能性はありますか。

> 過去の可能性について、may [might] や could などの助動詞を使って自分の判断を加える場合、それが過去の出来事についてのものであれば、「助動詞＋ have ＋過去分詞」の形をとる。

過去の確実性を表わす　Certainty

 Track 115

I **must have dropped** the bag in the movie theater.

The little toy **can't have cost** 12,000 yen. It's made of plastic.

The suitcase **couldn't have come open** by itself. We wrapped two straps around it.

1. Someone **must have seen** the accident. It's a busy street.
   誰かが、その事故を目撃したに違いない。交通量の多い通りだから。

2. Marco is a small guy. He **can't have eaten** the entire cake by himself.
   マルコは小柄な人だ。彼が一人でそのケーキをすべて食べたはずはない。

3. Akari **couldn't have been** at the party. She was on vacation in Nagoya.
   アカリがそのパーティーに参加していたとは思えない。休暇で名古屋にいたのだから。

> 確実性を表わす助動詞には、その度合いの高いものから must「…に違いない」、should「きっと…だろう」、can [could]「…のはずだ」、may [might]「…かもしれない」などがある。過去の出来事について判断を下す場合は、「助動詞＋ have ＋過去分詞」の形をとる。その場合、can よりも could、may よりも might の方が確信の度合いが低くなる。

I should have asked for permission before borrowing the bike.

Danny **shouldn't have bought** stock in that energy company.

Could the town **have prevented** the recent landslide?

1. We **should have booked** the tickets earlier. The price just went up.
   そのチケットはもっと早く予約するべきだった。たった今、価格が上がった。

2. I **could have enrolled** in the tango class, but I didn't.
   タンゴのクラスに参加の申し込めたはずだったが、そうしなかった。

3. I read your Facebook post. **Should** you **have revealed** so much about your personal life?
   あなたのフェイスブックへの投稿を読みました。あなたは自分の私生活をそんなに公開すべきだったのですか。

> 「…すべき［できたはず］だったがそうしなかった」という後悔の気持ちを表わすには、「should ＋ have ＋過去分詞」(…すべきだった)や「could have ＋過去分詞」(…できたはずなのに)を使う。

Grammar Exercises

 （　　）内の指示に従って、次の文を書き換えなさい。

[例] The fundraiser may have reached its goal. （否定文に）

　　→ The fundraiser may not have reached its goal.

1. A construction worker could have dug this hole. （疑問文に）

　_____

2. I shouldn't have changed my phone number. （肯定文に）

　_____

3. Tina must have locked the safe. （否定文に）

　_____

4. Might the dog have brought the shoe inside? （平叙文に）

　_____

5. We should have invited our new colleague to lunch. （疑問文に）

　_____

B 「助動詞＋完了時制」を使って、それぞれの文を完成させなさい。（　　）内の動詞を使うこと。

[例] The lock's combination must _____ been _____. (change)

　　→ The lock's combination must <u>have</u> been <u>changed</u>.

1. The amusement park's website may not _____ been _____ with the new opening hours. (update)

2. I should _____ _____ the revised schedule on the wall. (post)

3. The new employee couldn't _____ _____ the printer. (break)

4. Might a nail _____ _____ the tire puncture? (cause)

5. We could _____ _____ to a larger house, but we didn't. (move)

C 次の文を読み、その内容を正しく表しているものを A と B のどちらかから選びなさい。

1. This bank should have installed a wheelchair ramp years ago.

   (A) Years ago, a ramp was installed by the bank.

   (B) The bank did not install a ramp years ago.

2. The detective may have found an important clue in his investigation.

   (A) It's possible that the detective found an important clue.

   (B) An important clue was definitely found.

3. The berries must have been eaten by a deer.

   (A) It's almost certain that a deer ate the berries.

   (B) It's hard to say what happened to the berries.

Skill Building

A **Listening**　3つの文(A, B, C)を聞き、それぞれの内容と一致しているイラストの下にその記号を書きなさい。　🎧 Track 117

1. _____　　　2. _____　　　3. _____

B **Speaking**　次の会話文を読み、以下のリストから適切な単語を選んで空欄を埋めなさい。

| started | outside | have | get | should |

Cole:　Hi, I'm back from the farmer's market.

Ruby:　Hello. Did you ₁(　　　　　) some maple syrup from the Johnsons?

Cole:　No, they must ₂(　　　　　) sold out. Come to think of it, I ₃(　　　　　) have asked them to hold a bottle for me for next week.

Ruby:　It's all right. I drove by their farm the other day. They had a stall set up ₄(　　　　　), and I could have stopped to buy some syrup. I was in a hurry to get to work.

Cole:　It's all good. You know, I didn't see the Carsons' fruit stall today. They may have ₅(　　　　　) setting up at the market on Cape Street.

Ruby:　Interesting. We should check it out sometime.

質問の答えとして最も適切なものを選びなさい。

1. (　) Where did Ruby recently pass by?
   A: The Johnsons' farm　　　　B: A store on Cape Street
   C: The Carsons' home　　　　D: The new supermarket

2. (　) What does Cole regret?
   A: Getting to work late the other day
   B: Buying too much maple syrup at the market
   C: Not asking the Johnsons to hold something
   D: Forgetting to buy apples and oranges

C **Writing**　「助動詞＋現在完了形」を使って、それぞれの文を書き換えなさい。(　　)内の助動詞と動詞を使うこと。

1. The marathon runner has changed coaches. (might / have)

   _____

2. I made a mess in the kitchen. (should not / make)

   _____

3. Someone planted these flowers a few months ago. (must / plant)

   _____

A **Reading Passage**　次の英文を読み、（　　）内の正しいほうの単語を選びなさい。

July 15 was a special day for Orchard Hill. It was the small town's 100th birthday. ₁They (must / could) have had a regular parade. Instead, they decided to do something unique to make the day unforgettable.

First, everyone was encouraged to dress up like a townsperson from a century ago. People looked in their closets and attics for old hats, coats, and dresses. Jim Swanson found something special: an old suit that belonged to his great grandfather Martin. ₂Martin (shouldn't / must) have loved the suit, since it was well preserved. All day, people asked Jim to take pictures together.

Orchard Hill also wanted to honor the people who were near and dear to everyone's hearts. Leading the parade were teachers from kindergarten to high school. They were followed by doctors and nurses. First responders like firefighters and police officers also took part. The parade was a huge success, but organizers did have one regret. ₃They (should / mustn't) have ordered more ice cream. All of the ice cream sold out before 11:00!

NOTES　unforgettable「忘れられない」　encourage「…するよう促す」　townsperson「（町の）住民」　attic「屋根裏部屋」　preserve「保存する」　honor「称える」　near and dear「（人が）身近にいて大切な」　first responder「（災害や事故での）第一［初期］対応者」　regret「後悔（の気持ち）」

B **Comprehension**　それぞれの文の内容が正しければ T(true) を、誤りであれば F(false) を◯で囲みなさい。

1. In Orchard Hill, this year's parade was just like last year's.　　T　F

2. Jim Swanson bought a new suit of clothes to wear on July 15.　　T　F

3. Junior high school teachers were probably in the parade.　　T　F

C **Translation**　前ページの英文の中で、下線が引かれている文を日本語に訳しなさい。

1. _____

2. _____

3. _____

─────────────── **Reference Material** ───────────────

┌─「助動詞＋現在完了」の種類と用法　Variations of Modal + Present Perfect ─┐

1) can't have ＋ 過去分詞　「…したはずがない」
Kevin **can't have known** we were planning a surprise birthday party.

2) couldn't have ＋ 過去分詞　「…したはずがない」＊can't have よりも控えめで、よく使われる
Water officials said they **couldn't have prevented** the flood.

3) could have ＋ 過去分詞　　「…したかもしれない」＊(×)「can have ＋ 過去分詞」という形はない
I apologize. I **could have done** a better job explaining the product's features.

4) may have ＋ 過去分詞　　「…したかもしれない」
The dry cleaner **may have forgotten** to give me one of my shirts.

5) might have ＋ 過去分詞　　「もしかして…したかもしれない」＊may have よりも可能性が低い
I **might have left** my hat at the coffee shop.

6) must have ＋ 過去分詞　　「…したにちがいない」
The cat **must have jumped** over the backyard fence.

7) ought to have ＋ 過去分詞　「…したはず」／「…すべきだった（のに実際にはしなかった）」
I **ought to have bought** an extra bag of bagels for my sister.

8) ought not to have ＋ 過去分詞　「…すべきではなかったのに（した）」
The teacher said you **ought not to have brought** the toy to school.

9) should have ＋ 過去分詞　「…したはず」／「…すべきだった（のに実際にはしなかった）」
You **should have told** me you needed help repairing the barn.

10) should not have ＋ 過去分詞　「…すべきではなかったのに（した）」
The store **should not have listed** the item for sale online since it was out of stock.

11) need not have ＋ 過去分詞　　「…する必要はなかったのに（した）」＊主にイギリス英語
They **need not have sent** over a repair person. The copier is working fine.

181

LikeとAs　(Like and As) Track 118

The little boy walks **like** a duck.

This metal bar feels **as** cold **as** a stone.

It looks **like** the bottle leaked during shipping.

1. I love all kinds of desserts, **like** cake, cookies, and ice cream.
   私は、ケーキ、クッキー、アイスクリームなど、どんなデザートも大好きです。

2. There are cracks in the wall. It's the same kind of problem **as** the other warehouse.
   壁にいくつか割れ目がある。これは、ほかの倉庫であったのと同じような問題だ。

3. Doesn't your mother work **as** a salesperson at a department store?
   あなたのお母さんは、デパートの販売員として働いているのではないですか。

> as も like も、文脈によって異なる品詞として使われ意味も異なる。接続詞の as は「…と同じくらいの」という意味を表わし、前置詞の as は「…として」という意味になる。like は動詞なら「…が好き」だが、前置詞としては「…のような [に]」という意味で使われる。

DuringとWhile　(During and While) Track 119

I almost fell asleep **during** the speech.

While my dad cooked, I set the dinner table.

After a **while**, the car alarm stopped.

1. **During** the rainy season, I carry an umbrella everywhere.
   雨季の間は、私はどこへ行くにも傘を持ち歩きます。

2. We've been here a long **while**, and there's still no sign of Fumiko.
   私たちは長い間ここにいるが、まだフミコが現れる気配がない。

3. Do you always read a book **while** waiting for the train?
   列車を待っている間、あなたはいつも本を読むのですか。

> どちらも一定の期間を表わすために使われるが、during は前置詞なので名詞（句）が続く。while は接続詞なので文が続くが、主語が主節のものと同じ場合は 3. の文のように「主語＋be 動詞」を省略できる。また、while は名詞として「時間、期間」という意味もある。

SuchとSo (Such and So)

 Track 120

You are **such** a good listener.

These blueberries taste **so** good!

It was **so** cold that I put on a jacket.

1. We had **such** a great time at the festival.
   私たちは、そのお祭りでとても楽しい時間を過ごしました。

2. Christine did **such** a good job that she was given a bonus.
   クリスティンはとてもいい仕事をしたので、ボーナスを与えられた。

3. The store has **so** many hats. I can't decide which one to get.
   その店はたくさんの帽子を置いている。私はどれを買うべきか決めることができない。

---

such は主に形容詞として名詞（句）の前で「そのような、たいへんな」、so は副詞として形容詞の前で「そんなに、とても」の意味を表わす。どちらも後に続く語句を強調するために使われる。2 の文は「such ＋名詞句＋ that ...」の構文で「とても…なので…」という意味になる。

Grammar Exercises

A （　）内の正しい語を選び、文を完成させなさい。

1. Does that sound (like / as) a helicopter to you?

2. What are you going to do (while / during) summer vacation?

3. The juice is (so / such) sweet because it has pineapples in it.

4. Samantha's grandmother used to say to her, "You look as pretty (as / like) a picture."

5. (During / While) we're waiting for Cleo, tell me about your weekend.

6. After winning the match, the ping pong player was (such / so) excited that she jumped up and down.

7. The store has everything you need for your kitchen, (like / as) pots, knives, and cutting boards.

8. That was (such / so) a good movie. I want to see it again.

B 次の文のあとに続く表現の記号を、空欄に書き入れなさい。

1. To move the big rock, he pushed as _____

2. Do you usually try to sleep _____

3. We were surprised that the beach _____

4. Is it all right if I put my clothes _____

5. The magic show was such a success _____

(A) during long flights?

(B) that the promoter added more dates.

(C) away while we talk?

(D) hard as he could.

(E) was so crowded today.

C 次の文を読み、その内容を正しく表しているものを A と B のどちらかから選びなさい。

1. As the weather was poor, Joe took a train instead of riding his bike.
   (A) Joe always rides his bike, even in bad weather.
   (B) Because of the weather, Joe decided not to ride his bike.

2. While waiting for meals, guests can listen to a live band and dance.
   (A) If guests want, they can dance before they eat.
   (B) The band does not play when the restaurant is open.

3. The low-budget movie was so good that it won several awards.
   (A) The movie had a chance to win awards but wasn't successful.
   (B) Even though the movie had a small budget, it was award-winning.

--- **Skill Building** ---

A **Listening** 3つの文(A, B, C)を聞き、それぞれの内容と一致しているイラストの下にその記号を書きなさい。 🎧 Track 121

1. _____

2. _____

3. _____

B **Speaking**　次の会話文を読み、以下のリストから適切な単語を選んで空欄を埋めなさい。

during	as	like	such	so

Felix:　　Your uncle was ₁(　　　　　) generous with his time when I was looking for an apartment to rent. It was ₂(　　　　　) a big help, and I want to get him a gift to say thanks. Any ideas?

Connie:　Hmm...Uncle Jack loves European desserts ₃(　　　　　) cookies and pastries — oh, and especially Black Forest cake.

Felix:　　Interesting. My friend Judy works ₄(　　　　　) a server at a German restaurant. They have a bakery, too.

Connie:　There you go. I'm sure he'll like whatever you give him.

Felix:　　I hope so. I'll stop by the bakery ₅(　　　　　) my lunch break.

質問の答えとして最も適切なものを選びなさい。

1. (　　) Why does Felix want to give Connie's Uncle Jack a gift?
　　　A: Jack gave Felix's friend a job at a restaurant.
　　　B: Jack helped Felix find somewhere to live.
　　　C: Jack was very generous to Connie recently.
　　　D: Jack brought back nice presents from Germany.

2. (　　) What kind of gift does Connie recommend?
　　　A: Something to eat　　　　　B: Something to read
　　　C: Something to watch　　　　D: Something to wear

C **Writing**　(　　) 内の語句を並べ替え、正しい文を作りなさい。

1. This (as / feather / flag is / as a / light).

_____

2. I'll (in / while / be finished / a little / cooking dinner).

_____

3. The (so / couldn't move / train was / that we / crowded).

_____

Reading Passage　次の英文を読み、（　　）内の正しいほうの単語を選びなさい。

In recent years, we have learned a great deal about animal friendships. Many people once thought dogs and cats were natural enemies. ₁<u>Likewise, who could have imagined different species (as / like) donkeys and geese becoming friends?</u> Thanks to social media, animal lovers are sharing stories and videos which are changing our hearts and minds.

It's common for people to self-identify as "cat lovers" or "dog people." ₂<u>Yet, after cats and dogs live together for a (while / during), they often enjoy sharing a home.</u> In online videos, we can see kittens introduced to adult dogs. Dogs may show love, compassion, and even motherly affection. Rather than acting as enemies, they become close friends.

There are also heart-warming stories of lonely or mistreated rescue animals finding happiness. ₃<u>Moving to a new home makes (such / so) a big difference.</u> The animals are shown love and kindness, and multi-species friendships form. They may involve common animals like pigs and horses, as well as more exotic species like parrots and iguanas.

NOTES　likewise「（それと）同様に」　goose「ガチョウ（複数形：geese）」　thanks to「…のおかげで」　self-identify「自分を…だと自認する」　compassion「思いやり」　mistreat「虐待する」　rescue animal「保護された動物」　species「（動物の）種」　exotic「珍しい」

B **Comprehension**　それぞれの文の内容が正しければ T(true) を、誤りであれば F(false) を○で囲みなさい。

1. Social media is helping change how we think about animals.　　T　F

2. Cats and dogs never become good friends.　　T　F

3. In a rescue home, a parrot might live with a pig.　　T　F

C **Translation**　前ページの英文の中で、下線が引かれている文を日本語に訳しなさい。

1. _____

2. _____

3. _____

─── Reference Material ───

1) as long as / as far as

1. **As long as** you wear your headphones, you can listen to music in the library.
2. **As far as** I remember, there isn't anywhere to park near the aquarium.

どちらも「…する限り」という意味だが、as long as は条件を示すときに使うので「…ならば、…さえすれば」と言い換えられる。as far as は範囲を表すときに使うので「…の範囲では」と言い換えられる。

2) if / whether

1. Let me know **if** you have any questions.
2. **Whether** we can reach the sales target depends on our fourth quarter performance.

どちらも「…かどうか」という意味を表わす接続詞として名詞節を作る用法がある。したがって、ask, doubt, know, learn, see, tell, wonder などの目的語として使うことができる。ただし、whether が導く節は主語として文の先頭に置いたり、補語の位置に置いたりすることができるのに対し、if にはその用法はない。

3) by / until [till]

1. It's critical that we complete the prototype **by** next month.
2. Rather than wait **until** Friday, my client would like to sign the papers today.

by も until [till] も「…まで」という意味だが、by は「…までに(する)」という期限・締め切りを表わし、until [till] は,「その時点まで同じ状態が続く」ことを表わす。また、by は前置詞で、うしろに名詞（句）を伴うが、until [till] は前置詞だけではなく接続詞の用法もあるので、うしろに節が続いて副詞節になることができる。

4) unless / if not

1. **Unless** something unexpected happens, I'll see you tomorrow.
   = **If** something unexpected does **not** happen, I'll see you tomorrow.
2. I'll be surprised **if** Ken **doesn't** come to the party tomorrow.
   (×) I'll be surprised **unless** Ken comes to the party tomorrow.

unless は「…でない限りは」と条件の範囲を示す表現であるのに対し、if not は「もし…しなければ」という意味。unless と if not が置き換え可能なこともあるが、そうでない場合もあるので注意。

Grammar Plus【Second Edition】 　　　　　　　　　　　[B-943]
大学英語『グラマー・プラス』【改訂新版】
1 刷　2023年2月13日

著　者　　アンドルー E. ベネット　　　Andrew E. Bennett
　　　　　小宮　徹　　　　　　　　　　Toru Komiya
発行者　　南雲　一範　Kazunori Nagumo
発行所　　株式会社　南雲堂
　　　　　〒162-0801　東京都新宿区山吹町361
　　　　　NAN'UN-DO Co., Ltd.
　　　　　361 Yamabuki-cho, Shinjuku-ku, Tokyo 162-0801, Japan
　　　　　振替口座：00160-0-46863
　　　　　TEL: 03-3268-2311（代表）／FAX: 03-3269-2486
　　　　　編集者　加藤　敦
製　版　　Andrew E. Bennett
イラスト　Irene Fu
装　丁　　Irene Fu
検　印　　省　略
コード　　ISBN978-4-523-17943-6　C0082
　　　　　　　　　　　　　　　　　　　　　　　　　Printed in Japan

E-mail　nanundo@post.email.ne.jp
URL　https://www.nanun-do.co.jp/